Circles of Thorns

CIRCLES OF THORNS

*Hieronymous Bosch
and Being Human*

Justin Lewis-Anthony

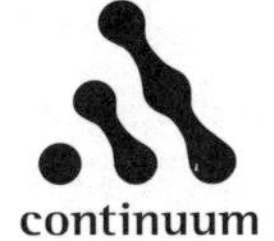

continuum

Continuum
The Tower Building, 11 York Road, London SE1 7NX
80 Maiden Lane, Suite 704, New York NY 10038

www.continuumbooks.com

First published 2008

British Library Cataloguing-in-Publication Data
A catalogue record for this book is available from the British Library.

ISBN: 978-1-9062-8621-7

Typeset by Kenneth Burnley, Wirral, Cheshire
Printed and bound in Great Britain by MPG Books Ltd, Bodmin, Cornwall

Contents

For

Siân,

who deserves far more

than just a book.

Introduction

In November 2006, the week before Advent Sunday, I had a nervous breakdown. It was something that had been coming for a long time, and I haven't completely 'recovered' even now. I spent ten months away from work, wholly missing the great festivals of the Church year: Christmas, Easter and Pentecost.

Time passed by very quickly: I was surprised by the arrival of spring, when just a moment before I had been preparing for winter. Time passed by very slowly: each day was very much like the one before, and the daily minor tasks (getting up, getting dressed, eating, household chores) were Herculean efforts that never ended. It was a strange 'in-between' time, halfway between nothing and nowhere.

At first, the nature of my breakdown meant I was unable to concentrate on anything. Depression frequently shows itself through disturbed sleep patterns, disturbed appetite, fatigue, and the wonderfully named anhedonia, the inability to take pleasure in previously satisfying activities. For me, one of the strongest forms of this anhedonia was the inability to concentrate. When concerned friends asked me if I was reading anything, I had a flippant answer, ready prepared to protect myself against further, closer, harder examination: 'Yes, I've been reading lots of detective novels, but I can't take in what I read. That's okay, because when I'm well, I can reread the books to find out whodunnit.'

Along with a loss of concentration went loss of prayer. It wasn't that I couldn't remember the techniques of prayer; where and how I should sit, what words I could use, the passages of the Bible upon which I could focus my prayers. The techniques of prayer were still open to me. However, as Christopher Jamison has so wisely taught, prayer is more than technique: it is not just something we *do*, but rather something we *are*. This deeper, richer understanding of prayer is hard enough to hold onto at the best of times. Even when we are well, we all experience constant yammering in our consciousness and our unconscious, what Christopher Jamison calls 'the noises inside my head'. He doesn't mean auditory hallucinations experienced by someone with a psychotic condition, rather 'the simpler phenomenon of thoughts racing in all directions at once'. He goes on to describe the requirements for prayer: 'To empty our heads of all thoughts, words and images is almost impossible; yet somehow these distressing internal noises need to become gentle internal sounds.'[1]

This 'emptying' was impossible for me. Some people experience depression as a great deadening of emotion: I experienced it as a great unleashing. I don't mean that I was manic, suffering from bipolar disorder. Rather, every potential emotion which I could have felt in everyday life, but which, in a normal mental condition would have been too small or too fleeting to notice, in my depression actually arrived at the forefront of my mind, demanding attention. With such a sea of emotions sloshing around, there was too much of me for God to get a look in. Being depressed pushed out the possibility of being still in the presence of God.

I found my way back to prayer through two gifts. The first was something I could hold on to: a set of prayer beads from a parishioner and friend. They swiftly became the must-have thing I took with me wherever I went, even though I couldn't say my prayers with them: the first time I used the beads I even managed to forget the words of the Lord's Prayer. However, just holding the 33 beads, clicking through them, reminded me that once I could pray, and that even then others were praying. Gradually the memory became something in the present again, and so the beads led me gently back to a regular sitting in the presence of God.

The second gift was not something that I could ever hold on to without being arrested, a gift from a man who died almost 500 years ago: a painting. I visited the gallery in which the painting is shown; I kept a postcard of it near my bed. Eventually, from the gallery's website, I printed a smaller version, small enough to slip inside a notebook, which I carried wherever I went. As I recovered, I realized that this painting had held before me profound insights into the nature of being human, our frailties, our needs, our desires and sins and disappointments. The insights were all the more profound for the *way* in which the message was conveyed and the still, loving, presence at the heart of the painting. The painting is, as I say, 500 years old, but it is passionately modern. It is a 'religious' painting, from a culture we find almost impossible to imagine, let alone understand. But, with a little help, and a little time, I believe the painting can speak to us today, teaching us what it means to be more fully human

The painting is *Christ Mocked* (*The Crowning with Thorns*) by Hieronymus Bosch in the National Gallery in London, and this book is a journey accompanied by the painting, the artist's vision of one event in history and its continued meaning, and an understanding of what it means to be truly human, truly alive. The journey will not be one that follows a straight line, for, as we shall see, the artist didn't paint or think in straight lines, and the depths and truths of the Christian story are not to be found in straight lines. The journey will be rather a series of circles, each skimming a different part of the ocean of meaning contained in the painting, drawn around the suffering of Christ and the moment in his Passion when he received the mockery of the Roman soldiers, in which he was crowned with thorns. We will move in five circles, coming closer every time to the still centre of the painting. We will pass from 'Politics', in which we see Bosch's exploration of the part that power had to play in the death of Jesus; to 'Elements', where his scientific understanding of the universe shows the cosmic significance of the Passion; to 'Temperaments', in which Bosch shows us a vision of the complexity of human character and its complicity in Jesus's suffering; to 'Devotions', where the call to renewal, of faith and spirituality and Church, in Bosch's day finds an echo in our own; to 'Quiddity' where we finally reach our beginning and our ending, our fulfilment and our transformation. The still centre of the painting is, of course, Christ himself.

Although the painting shows an episode from Christ's Passion, it is not a painting (and neither is this a book) just for Lent or Holy Week. Bosch was too great a painter to limit himself to one season of the Church year, and neither should we. Rather, by choosing to depict in the way he did a single moment from one spring day 1,500 years before his time, Bosch shows us the whole Christian story, its challenge and its comfort. This painting is for Good Friday, and for Easter Day; it is crucifixion and resurrection. It is for Christmas and Advent, for it is Incarnation and judgement. It is for all the days of the year (and our lives) that go without special names. It is a painting of a death, but also a painting of an invitation to life. It is a point of departure on life's pilgrimage and the place to which we journey. To understand the painting, and to take up the invitation with which it presents us, is to undertake the task of being human.

Note

1   Christopher Jamison, *Finding Sanctuary: Monastic steps for everyday life* (London: Weidenfeld & Nicholson, 2006) p. 35.

An Unrelenting Gaze in WC1

Three minutes from Charing Cross station, on the northern, pedestrianized, side of Trafalgar Square, stands the National Gallery. It is not a particularly distinguished building (likened, when it was first built in the 1830s, to a pepperpot) but it contains one of the great collections of art in the world.

Amongst the paintings from the Netherlands, 1500–30, is the National Gallery's single example of the work of that most mysterious artist, Jeroen van Aken, El Bosco, Hieronymus Bosch. *Christ Mocked*, or *The Crowning with Thorns*, is not a very large painting, slightly less than 74 cm by 60 cm (about two and a half by two feet). The frame is plain for its company and for the time it was painted: simple gold and black bands. There is nothing ostentatious about it, nothing that shouts out the importance of the subject matter, the cleverness of the artist's interpretation, the sophistication of his technique, or the relevance of its role in the history of Western art. The painting is not dynamic; I don't sense a momentary capture of a series of movements. The eyes don't even follow me around the room. In a word, Bosch's painting is not *flash*.

Five figures are depicted. There is no problem identifying the only figure whose eyes look out at me: it is Christ, depicted conventionally enough, with beard and long hair in a lustrous auburn. His beard is thin, divided faintly into a fork beneath his chin. His head is inclined to his right, although not at an extreme angle: he looks more quizzical than uncomfortable.

There is no halo, no nimbus of heavenly light. Surrounding him are four figures, each of whom gazes intently upon Christ: eye-lines all converge on Christ's own eyes. They are looking at him: he is looking at me.

In the upper left, looming above Christ, is a gaunt, dark-haired man, dressed in forest green. Through his turban is stuck a curious blunt-edged arrow, as if ready to be used in an instant. In his hands, only one of which we can see, protected by shining dark grey elbow gauntlets, he is holding a crown of thorns. He is about to place it on Christ's head, and, although it doesn't yet touch the head, when it does it will be pushed down with some force. The green man's mouth is gripped with tight effort. The circle of thorns hovers behind Christ's head like a kind of vicious halo.

In the upper right, again set above Christ, is another military figure, one dressed in dark colours, a black fur hat, a metal collar with spikes around his neck, a dark blue-grey collar resting on his shoulders, and, just visible behind his left hand, which clutches a birch-wood staff, a red jerkin (the metal disk below his left shoulder is called a *besagew*, and was intended to protect a soldier's armpit). His right hand reaches around Christ's shoulders; we can see the fingers resting on Christ's right side, just beneath the gauntlet of the green man. The dark man's face is turned towards Christ, with a look of . . . what? Compassion, concern, involvement? The dark man is painted with such particularity, with no hint of caricature, that I feel I would recognize him if I met him on the street. His face is *modern*. And, although he looks concerned, the overall effect of his presence is somehow threatening.

In the lower right corner is a figure in pale red, almost rose. He is reaching up from his position on the extreme right of the panel, his face in profile, both hands extending to grasp Christ's robe. At first I think he is holding Christ's hand, hidden behind the robe, but, looking carefully, I can see that both Christ's hands are beneath the man in rose's arms, resting at peace, one above the other on his thigh, which is exposed in a crumple of the linen. There is an intense stare on the face of the man in rose, his head framed by a dark hood that seems to form part of an overgarment. Sometimes it looks as if he is slipping away from the others in the group, falling into an unseen hole in that corner of the picture. When I notice that, his grasp on Christ's robe seems all the more physical, rough in its intensity.

The lower left corner is filled by a man in blue, who wears a red headdress weighed down with metal baubles that look like tiny prickly stars. Again, I see his face in profile, and whereas the man in rose is dark-haired and dark-featured, the blue man is old. His hair, sticking out from under his headdress, is white, and he has a thin wispy beard. His eyes (or at least the eye I can see) are shining; and with his reddish nose and open mouth, jaw jutting out slightly, there is a curious sense that he has a cold, and is about to sneeze. The shining eyes are watering. His left hand holds a staff, this one of dark, worn, wood, which points back to him. His right hand reaches out and touches Christ, where the latter's hands rest on his knee. There is something slightly lascivious about his appearance and actions. He is not a comfortable character to observe closely.

That is all there is to see in the painting. There is no background, no foreground. The four outer figures entirely fill the sides of the panel, the two lower ones entirely fill the bottom. Only above the heads of the two upper figures (the green man and the dark man), around the head of Christ and through the thorns of the crown, can we see anything that is neither human, nor clothing: a dark grey background, very, very faintly streaked with softer peach stripes (although I have to look very closely to see those). It is almost as if Bosch is telling us that there is *nothing* else to look at: he doesn't want us to be distracted from the event and people in the foreground. He wants my gaze, our gaze, to be as unrelenting as the gazes of the four tormentors.

An unrelenting gaze; a fierce obligation to look. What is there to see in this painting? Is there anything beyond its five characters? How can we best 'read' what Bosch has set before us?

We cannot approach these questions head-on: the intensity of the gaze would be too much for us, like rabbits caught in the headlights. We need to come up to the questions in a round-about way: we need to circle ourselves about, taking what we learn from each circle into the next until we find ourselves at the heart of the painting, at the answer to the questions. The first circle will be the easiest to draw out, answering the most obvious questions: who are these men, why are they dressed so strangely, so unlike our idea of Roman soldiers? We find, therefore, that our first circle leads us into a study of politics and power.

Circle 1: Politics

Michael Portillo, once a politician, was disturbed by the news that the leader of the Conservative party hoped to send his daughter to a Church of England school. Portillo described his unease in a column for the *Sunday Times*, with the headline 'If God is talking to you, too, Mr Cameron – don't listen'. Cameron's desire for his daughter's education was an entirely suspect thing because it seemed to undermine, according to Portillo, the Elizabethan settlement (the way in which Elizabeth I managed to control and curb the religious disputes that had so disfigured the reigns of her father, brother and sister).

> If today the Church of England is wishy-washy and middle-of-the-road, that is no accident. It is the long-term result of Elizabeth's design. Britain has benefited enormously from a weak clergy that has mainly remained aloft from politics. Britain's established church, headed by the monarch, has made few demands of our leaders or people.

This is not a bad thing, in Portillo's sight, for he concluded his argument with this assertion that 'men of power who take instruction from unseen forces are essentially fanatics'.[1]

Mr Portillo's point of view is shared by many influential politicians. Alistair Campbell, Tony Blair's press secretary, famously discouraged the then-prime minister from responding to a question about the relationship between faith and politics: 'We don't do God,' was Campbell's now proverbial refusal. We should keep God and politics well apart, suggests Portillo, so as not to be overwhelmed by 'theocrats, religious leaders or fanatics citing holy texts . . . [dictating] . . . violent actions'.

It would be interesting to know if Michael Portillo likes our painting by Bosch. When he looks upon it does he see 'a good way, perhaps the best way, to impart a sense of right and wrong to children' or does he see religion and politics hopelessly muddled? I think he would be profoundly suspicious of the painting, because our first circle around *Christ Mocked* shows politics right at the heart of religion. For Bosch, religion is politics and politics is religion.

Strangely, Bosch makes this (nowadays) radical statement by producing an essentially conservative painting. I don't mean by this that he has painted the virtues of small government, fiscal responsibility and opposition to the euro; I mean, rather, that Bosch used a style of painting, a way of arranging his subject matter, that was familiar to his viewers, which they had seen many times before, and which they would be able to 'read' straight off the surface. By following a convention, Bosch could convey his meaning clearly. Our painting's first viewers would have immediately understood the Circle of politics; the twentieth-century viewer, by contrast, needs to do a little more work, and to understand what were the conventions of Bosch's style.

The first thing to remember when looking at Bosch's painting is that, with his Lowlands[2] style, what you get is not what you see, at least not with a first or second glance. His style had its origins in illuminated manuscripts. These works of art in book form were designed to be held close, studied as much and as closely as the text of the book itself. A richness of colour and a wealth of detail were needed in the picture, to entrance and divert the eye. When the manuscript illuminators moved to the larger medium of painting they took their assumptions and techniques with them. People expected the same sort of richness and detail in their paintings. 'The secret of holding the attention through such an exhaustive test lay not in novelty, which soon palls, but in meeting the anticipated exposure to examination by a concentration equal in intensity.'[3]

We can see this richness and detail in the great triptych paintings for which Bosch is most famous: *The Hay Wain*, *The Garden of Earthly Delights* or *The Ship of Fools*. At first glance, we might think they are no more than a sort of pornographic 'Where's Wally'; at second glance it is possible for us to see the deeper structures of the painting, the relationship of the objects depicted, the layers of pigmentation and the colour palette, all these things rewarding our concentrated gaze. The paintings' secrets open out before us like a treasure chest.

But, like the treasure hunter, we need clues to follow in the hunt for the treasure. In Bosch's day the trail of artistic clues was made up by conventions of style. The educated viewer, recognizing the conventions, could 'tick off' the clues in whatever scene the artist had made: a picture of the crucifixion required a pelican in the background (the pelican was a symbol of the crucifixion because it was believed the mother pelican fed her chicks on blood pecked from her own breast); a scene of a scholar needed an owl in the frame (the owl, curiously, could be a symbol either of learning or of evil). In paintings of the Passion, the viewer would expect to see representations of the *Arma Christi*, the instruments of the Passion. It wasn't just a case of no crucifixion without resurrection, no resurrection without crucifixion: there would be no crucifixion without the scourge, the crown of thorns, the robe, the hammer, the nails.[4] Sure enough, in our painting we can see one instrument: the crown of thorns. But what other conventions has Bosch followed? Where is the richness of detail in our painting? We have just five men, arranged claustrophobically, with no other detail. What do we get from the second or third glance?

Look at the picture again, and consider the way Bosch has arranged his five figures: Christ in the centre, surrounded by the four tormentors. In illuminated capitals of the late Middle Ages (where the first letter of a section of text is wonderfully and elaborately decorated) it had become customary to place four figures around the central figure of Christ (either his head, crowned with halo or thorns, or the whole body upon the cross).[5] Each of these surrounding figures was a type, representing the breadth of medieval society: clockwise from top left, they were usually a king (the rulers), a bishop (the churchmen), a merchant (the bourgeoisie) and a peasant. Is it possible to read the four tormentors of our painting in a similar way?

Look again at the green man, in the top left corner of the painting. He is dressed as a soldier, wearing armour, we presume, under his green robe— we can see one gauntlet clearly. Through his turban is placed a crossbow arrow. Is this enough evidence to mark him as a representative of a king?

There is another painting of the mocking of Christ, now in the Escorial in Madrid, which was long thought to be by Bosch.[6] In that painting is another tormentor with an arrow through his hat: this tormentor wears a badge, the double-headed eagle of the Holy Roman Empire. Emperor Maximilian I, head of the Habsburg family, was *the* secular ruler of Bosch's day, ruler of the European superpower. Is Bosch wanting us to make the connection with our arrow-hatted man? There is another, more direct, clue that the green man stands for secular power: he holds the crown. It is the green man who is about to place the crown upon Christ's head. The right to crown kings, determining the next ruler, was a right jealously fought over between Church and state. Here, the

Emperor's man is depicted exercising the sovereign power in a mock coronation.

If the green man is the Emperor's servant, then Bosch was being very daring. Today we might think the Habsburgs were a family limited to Hungary and Austria, small countries, far away. In Bosch's day the Habsburgs ruled, either directly or through marriage alliances, Austria, Bohemia, Spain, the Lowlands, and the duchy of Burgundy (vast swathes of present-day France). Maximilian I, through ingenuity, diplomacy and skilled marriage negotiations, had hugely expanded his family's power, first by wedding Mary of Burgundy, and then by marrying off his son to the Infanta of Spain (daughter of Ferdinand and Isabella), the unfortunate Juana the Mad. Maximilian's grandson, Charles V, became Holy Roman Emperor two years after Bosch's death, and, through inheritance from his maternal grandparents, controlled most of the New World. In short, in Bosch's day the Habsburgs were a family on the up.

Maximilian's son (and Charles's father), Philip the Handsome, was always on the lookout for talented painters. His attention was drawn to the able painter from Den Bosch, a town ruled through his Netherlandish regency. In 1504 he commissioned Bosch to paint a *Last Judgement* (possibly the *Last Judgement* now in the Akademie der Bildenden Künste in Vienna), and became an enthusiastic collector of Bosch's work. And yet Bosch chose to include as one of Christ's tormentors a not-so-veiled representation of Habsburg power. What was he thinking of?

Sometimes we are told that politics is the realistic science: there is no room for naivety or sentiment in working the art of the possible. We are told this, usually, when something unpleasant or unethical is about to be done in our name. Our liberties, our way of life, our system of government, is dependent on violent things being done by violent people. Bosch here shows the government of his day as good as complicit in Christ's torture, and he refuses to allow us to look away. What wickedness do we condone by looking away? But we can't afford the moral luxury of proclaiming 'not in my name' and thinking that lets us off the hook. Bosch here tells us that there is no neutral place to stand, no safe haven, when it comes to the ways of the world. The men and systems we look to for our protection may be the ones perpetuating the violence. As Bob Dylan wrote, 'We live in a political world / Love don't have any place. We're living in times where men commit crimes / And crime don't have a face.'[7]

There is another soldier in the painting, the dark man in the top right corner. Perhaps the first thing we notice about him is the vicious collar of spikes around his neck, but then our eyes are drawn by the line of the collar, past its buckle, to the spray of oak leaves pinned to his great fur hat. There is nothing cryptic about this badge. The oak leaf was known throughout Europe as the badge, the *impresa*, of one of the great families of Italy, the della Roveres.[8] From obscure origins in Liguria (the tiny strip of land between France, the Alps and the Mediterranean around Genoa), they rose to produce two popes: Francesco della Rovere, Pope Sixtus IV (1471–84), and Sixtus's nephew Guiliano della Rovere (1443–1513), who became Pope Julius II in 1503.

Julius II was, depending on your point of view, either the greatest Pope of his age and one of the great princes of European history, or an unmitigated disaster for Church and state. On the one hand, he was a patron of the arts; laying the foundation stone for the new basilica of St Peter in Rome, commissioning Michelangelo Buonarroti to paint the ceiling of the Sistine Chapel and Raphael to paint the frescos of the Vatican Palace. On the other hand, Julius sought to fix his control over the Papal States in Italy by eliminating his great rivals, the Borgias (also 'no better than they oughta'), neutralizing the power of the Venetian republic, and removing French control of the Italian peninsula. It is no coincidence that the Swiss Guard, the papal bodyguard, was founded by Julius, and that he is most commonly known as 'the warrior pope'. One historian, Jacob Burckhardt, called him the 'saviour of the papacy', another, Leopold von Ranke, said of him that 'even depravity may have its perfection'.[9]

This, unsurprisingly, had its effect upon the religious life of Rome and the whole of Europe. Michelangelo, who spent so much of his life working for (and being paid by) Julius, even wrote a sonnet lamenting how low things had become in Rome:

> Here helms and swords are made of chalices:
> The blood of Christ is sold so much the quart:
> His cross and thorns are spears and shields; and short
> Must be the time 'ere even his patience cease.
> Nay let him come no more to raise the fees
> Of this foul sacrilege beyond report!
> For Rome still flays and sells him at the court,
> Where paths are closed to virtue's fair increase.[10]

This is perhaps why Bosch chose not to depict the 'clergy corner' tormentor in clerical robes. He is telling us that the clergy of Europe have given themselves over to the control of the warrior pope and his armies. The sword that Jesus told Peter to sheath at his arrest (Matthew 26.52) has been picked up by Julius and his representative in our painting.

There is another clue to the dark man standing for the political power of the Church. It is the object that first caught our eye: his collar. It cannot be part of his armour or weaponry; what possible use is such a spiked collar? It would be no use for a soldier, but it would do for a dog. Does it not look like the collar of a particularly fierce dog? Bosch wasn't making a simple joke about dog collars and clerical collars: a white band at the neck as the badge of clergymen was an English invention in the nineteenth century, and 'dog collar' only became a nickname for clergy dress in the 1860s. But there was a group of clergy in Bosch's day who had a canine connection: the Order of Preachers, also known as the Blackfriars. Their informal name was Dominicans, after their founder St Dominic, and 'Dominican' can be read as the two Latin words *domini* and *canes*: the dogs of God. Dogs are noted for two things: faithful obedience and fierce aggression. The Dominicans gained a reputation for both, especially in the part they played in the inquisitions of late medieval and early modern Europe.

It is important to remember that in Bosch's lifetime there was no such thing as 'the Inquisition'. There was no pan-European office, famed for its 'surprise, ruthless efficiency, an almost fanatical devotion to the Pope'. Despite the imaginative power of Monty Python, the real thing was rather different: more localized, diffuse, and secular. In Bosch's day there was really only one local inquisition operating, set up by Pope Sixtus IV in 1483 to deal with the peculiar circumstances following the reconquest of Spain. Sixtus appointed as its head the pious and austere Tomás de Torquemada, a Dominican. In making his dark man wear a dog collar and the oak leaves of the della Rovere family, was Bosch hinting at the dangerous complicity between the Church and political power? Look at the expression on the dark man's face again. Although his brow is furrowed in compassionate consolation, and his arm rests lightly upon Jesus's shoulder, do you doubt that compassion and lightness will be transformed in the instant that the crown, hovering over Jesus's head, is pushed into place? Look at the way he grasps his staff, all exposed knuckles. If this staff is the 'reed' of Matthew 27.29, then in a moment it will become a mock sceptre in further humiliation for Jesus. If it is just a staff, then it will be used to beat and drive the prisoner to the place of his execution. The dark man, the soldier of the Church, is as guilty as any for the sufferings of Christ.

We have seen that Bosch's 'conservative style' didn't mean that he was a member of the Conservative party. Perhaps it then becomes tempting to lean the other way, to think that Bosch was a good *Guardian*-reading liberal. He has condemned the great powers of his day: the Empire and the Church. He has, in the words of that once true but increasingly hackneyed phrase, spoken truth to power.[11] But we cannot sign up Bosch to the liberal chattering classes: look at the other two tormentors in the picture: the man in rose and the old man. Here we are on dangerous ground, for there seems to be good reason to suppose that Bosch meant these two tormentors to stand for Jews and Muslims.

In the old tradition of the illuminated capital, the man in rose is placed in the position for the bourgeoisie; the burgher, the merchant. He is painted with a dark complexion; a large nose shown in profile; dark, bushy eyebrows; and a prominent jaw with a protruding lower lip. Just visible under his black hood is a wisp of hair, streaked dark red. These are all common enough signs for a Jew. In medieval iconography, Judas Iscariot was depicted with red hair, which in turn became known as 'Judas-coloured'. Even a modern film-maker, Martin Scorsese, in his film *The Last Temptation of Christ*, chose to give his Judas (played by Harvey Keitel) flaming red hair. We are confronted here with the unavoidable fact that, for most of European history, our culture has been unrepentantly anti-Semitic, and the posture of the man in rose depicts one of the vilest anti-Semitic libels of European history.

The man stretches up, lifting his arms high, and grasps Christ in both hands. This would have been read by Bosch's original viewers, I am sure, as a depiction of the libel of Jewish 'Host desecration'.

In the late Middle Ages, the theology of the Eucharist developed in richness and complexity. Scholars speculated on the what and the how and the why the Mass achieved the redemption of the faithful: what do we mean when we pray the words of the scriptures: 'This is my body that is for you. Do this in remembrance of me . . . This cup is the new covenant in my blood. Do this, as often as you drink it, in remembrance of me' (1 Corinthians 11.24f).[12]

The Fourth Lateran Council settled this speculation with the theory of transubstantiation: that the bread and wine by being prayed over by a priest, while retaining their outward appearance, were transformed in their real substance into the body and blood of Christ. Of course, if you believe that bread and wine actually become the body and blood, the very substance of your Saviour, then the bread and wine become very precious indeed. So there grew a positive paranoia for protecting the sacrament from abuse. The cup of wine was withheld from the laity because they might be confused by its 'winely form', and so fall into the temptation of drinking disrespectfully. Rumours grew about the wicked uses to which Jews and infidels would put the consecrated Hosts. In 1515 in Halle, Germany, Johann Pfefferkorn, a 'baptized Jew', confessed, after being tortured with red-hot pincers, to a number of crimes. These included poisoning wells, attempting to poison the Archbishop of Magdeburg, serving as a priest for 20 years 'although he had never been ordained or consecrated', and having 'stolen three consecrated hosts. He had kept one of them, martyring and piercing it. The other two he had sold to the Jews.' Following his confession, burning coals were raked about him until he was roasted to death.[13]

In what way does Bosch's depiction of the man in rose connect with the Host desecration libel? Well, Bosch depicts him as grasping at the body of Christ, the only one of the tormentors to do so (the green man is not touching Christ; the dark man's hand rests upon Christ's shoulders; the old man rests his hand upon Christ's lap). His arms are elevated in a way that would remind the painting's viewers of the elevation of the Host at the climax of the Mass. This liturgical action was a common subject for artists of the Middle Ages, particularly in the form of a painting of the legend of the Mass of St Gregory. Bosch himself painted a version in the grisaille outer panels of the *Adoration of the Magi* triptych now in the Prado. In this legend, we are told how St Gregory celebrated Mass, at which was present the woman who baked the bread. She refused to believe that her loaf could become the body of Christ. To answer her disbelief, Jesus, in the form of the Man of Sorrows, miraculously appeared above the altar at the elevation of the Host. It was a very popular theme: Jean Poyet, the great illuminator, painted a version of the legend in about 1500 for a Book of Hours, once owned by Henry VIII of England.[14] In it St Gregory's arms stretch up, holding the Host, a large white disc of bread. For the devout of the late Middle Ages there was literally no difference between the consecrated Host and the body of the Man of Sorrows above Gregory's hands. It is an image inescapably similar to the position of the man in rose.

A charitable, modern interpretation of the man in rose might be that Bosch wants us to recognize those who seek to grasp Christ, to use him in profane ways, and their sin is as great as the soldiers who originally crucified him. If the crime confessed by poor Pfefferkorn was commonly believed to happen in Bosch's day, no wonder he placed the Jew grasping at the body of Christ into the position traditionally held by the merchant-tormentor. Commerce and desecration combine.

But the charitable interpretation of the motives of Bosch cannot really be sustained in our day, after the culmination of years of European anti-Semitism in the Jewish Holocaust.

Rather, here we should learn a *negative* lesson from Bosch, and repudiate the beliefs behind the painting.

The Western European fear of the Jews was based on fantasy and fearfulness. There was another, more real threat to their society, represented by the fourth tormentor, the old man.

Painted on his red headdress is a crescent moon, the symbol of Islam: the old man represents the infidel in the East. In 1500 the threat posed by Islam to Europe was very real. The last remnant of Christendom in the East, the Byzantine Empire centred on Constantinople, had been conquered by Turkish invaders in 1453, when Bosch was a child. In the 50 years since the fall of Byzantium, the princes of the West had quarrelled among themselves while the Ottomans consolidated their power in the Balkans. In the decade and a half after Bosch's death, under Suleyman the Magnificent, the Ottomans took control of the Arab caliphates in Syria and Egypt. In 1526, the kingdom of Hungary, which had long regarded itself as the bulwark of Christendom against the Turk, was destroyed in the Battle of Mohács. The king of Hungary (nephew to the Holy Roman Emperor), five bishops, two archbishops, the nobility and 16,000 soldiers were all killed. The capital, Buda, was destroyed, and the Turks moved westwards. By 1529 they had laid siege to Vienna. In the hundred years from the fall of Constantinople, 'in south-eastern Europe . . . the Turks were a real and present source of terror to all ranks in society . . . it is impossible to understand the mood of sixteenth-century Europe without bearing in mind the deep anxiety inspired by the Ottoman Empire'.[15]

It is a weary, and inaccurate, commonplace to describe today the relationship between 'the West' and 'the Arab world' (or 'liberal democracies' and 'Islamo-fascist states', or 'Christianity' and 'Islam') as a 'clash of civilizations'. It is too soon, and I think there are too many other factors involved, for us to decide if this is an accurate description. There is, however, no question that it is an accurate description of what was happening in Europe in 1500. Not, note, a 'clash of religions': there were other factors involved. The development of nation states (centrally administered powers based upon defined geographical areas); pressure upon the Arab world from a westward-moving migration of Turkic tribes; securing of preferential trade routes to the Far East (certainly an important consideration for Venetian actions): all these combined with a real misunderstanding of and fearfulness for what was represented by Islam. The Muslims had been expelled from the western edge of Europe: it seemed very likely that they would be soon sweeping in from the east.

Which is why Bosch identified one of his tormentors with the Turk. For him the body of Christ was manifested in one way by the Christian kingdoms of Europe. Damage to Christendom was damage to the body of Christ, and the greatest threat to Christendom came from the Turk.

Europe in 1500 was at a crossroads, and its future survival was by no means guaranteed. The glories of Florence and Rome would matter not one whit if Christendom was lost. Political power in Bosch's day was shifting. The old certainties and the old centres of power were no longer holding. Within 50 years of Bosch's death, the world collapsed. The Spanish Netherlands rebelled against their rulers and the Eighty Years War began. The destruction, of property, people and society was incalculable.

Bearing all this in mind, thinking of the political situation of Europe in 1500, and thinking of the political situation in which we find ourselves today, we can see the significance of Bosch's decision to draw the circle of responsibility for Christ's suffering so widely. The painting says more than just 'J'accuse!'; Bosch forcefully states '*J'accuse tout le monde!*' All the world is culpable. The green man stands for the Holy Roman

Emperor, who in turn stands for princes and secular powers. The dark man stands for the papacy and the friars, who tear at the body of Christ through inquisition and by conducting themselves as princes. The man in rose stands for Jewry: those who attacked the body from the inside, and who use commerce to commodify Christ. The old man stands for the Turk at the gates of Europe, whose threat frightens Christendom and, through fear, depraves and corrupts the godly rule of the kingdom of Christ. It is as if Bosch says everyone in the known world has a part to play in Christ's torment; he asks us, where in this circle of sadism do you place yourself?

Bearing this in mind, we realize the weakest part of the painting is, paradoxically, the most potent. Christ in the centre is completely powerless in the face of the powers of the world. He does not protest, he does not resist, he does not rail against his captors; he does not tell them who he really is and what their wickedness will earn them. Rather, at rest, centred, he gazes at us, as if to ask us if we can follow in this path of loving detachment. Can we be strong in Christ's weakness? Can we remember that the Christian vocation is, in the words of Rowan Williams, 'to live out the weakness of Christ in our material lives so that the power which depends on nothing but its own glorious integrity can appear'.[16]

The danger for the body of Christ, and for us as its constituent members, is to think that we are an organization like any other, organized like any other, that operates power within and without itself, using the same systems of control as the secular princes. This is called 'being realistic'. Actually, it is more truly described as 'being damned'. I think, and perhaps Bosch thought, that the dark man, the attack dog of the papacy, is the tormentor most lost, most pitied by God and most in need of the redemption of Christ.

But the paradox deepens. The moment the tormentors inflict their humiliation upon Christ is also the beginning of their redemption. We can understand this best by remembering Jesus's teaching in the Sermon on the Mount. There, famously, he tells his listeners that 'if anyone strikes you on the right cheek, turn the other also . . . and if anyone forces you to go one mile, go also the second mile' (Matthew 5.39, 41).

This is not the advocacy of passivity in the face of violence. Walter Wink and Rowan Williams (again) have described it as something strong and active and whole:

> The slave stands there rather than going away and slowly turns his head. The peasant looks at the soldier and speaks to him, saying, 'I choose to go another mile.' The world of the aggressor, the master, is questioned because the person who is supposed to take no initiatives suddenly does. As Gandhi discovered, this is very frightening for most of those who exercise power. It is action that changes the terms of the relation, or at the very least says to the master that the world might be otherwise. It requires courage and imagination: it is essentially the decision not to be passive, not to be a victim, but equally not to avoid passivity by simply reproducing what's been done to you. It is always something of a miracle.[17]

Bosch paints the moment of the miracle. Do we have the trust to accept the working of the miracle in our lives?

There is one more layer of which we should be aware in this political circle of the painting: the sheer fact of Jesus's suffering. Today we call this treatment cruel and inhuman and, although it has been outlawed since 1949 in the various Geneva Conventions and since 1987 in the United Nations Convention against Torture and Other Cruel, Inhuman or Degrading Treatment or Punishment, it still continues. An occupying power, frustrated by the intransigence, the continued belligerence, the *stupidity*, of the occupied people, decides to show who's boss. Inflicting such treatment helps bolster the morale of the troops stationed a long way from home, surrounded by those who wish them harm. There is nothing new or surprising in this behaviour. The fact that we are still legislating against its occurrence two thousand years after the cruel treatment inflicted upon a criminal from Nazareth shows how ingrained it is in human nature.

Perhaps, though, at the beginning of the twenty-first century, depictions of the *public* humiliation of an enemy resonate more than before. For 150 years, the state (at least in Western democracies) conducted such activities behind closed doors. Once public executions ceased, justice, of whatever kind or quality, was a hidden thing. But, with the invention of digital cameras, mobile telephone cameras and the internet, once more the interrogation rooms and the torture rooms and the execution rooms have been exposed to public view. Publically, on the evening news if the pictures aren't too terrifying, or privately, via the internet, if they are, we can see what untrammelled state power over the individual looks like. Abu Ghraib and Guantanamo Bay are just the most blatant, recent, examples of something that has happened throughout history. The execution of Saddam Hussein was regretted, not because it happened, and neither because it happened in an undignified way, but because its indignities were filmed. The execution was condemned because his last minutes of life were broadcast to the world, as if exposure on television was something worse than hanging by a rope until your neck is broken and your head is wrenched off.

But *Christ Mocked* is not a piece of photo-journalism. There is nothing of the lurid intensity that we have come to associate with torture images. There is no blood. Jesus is not even bruised. Which leads to a puzzling question: which Gospel account has Bosch painted?[18]

Is it Matthew's, where Jesus is whipped and stripped,

dressed in the scarlet robe of a Roman soldier, crowned with thorns, given a reed for a sceptre, and mocked?

Is it Mark's account where, at the end of a trial, Jesus is beaten, and clothed in a purple cloak and crowned with thorns and the reed is used to beat him once more?

Is it Luke's account, where Jesus, despite his prophecy in Luke 18.33, is never scourged by the Romans and the mockery takes place in Herod's court, where he is verbally abused and dressed in a 'splendid' robe?

Is it John's account, where Jesus is beaten in the middle of his trial, in a naked show of tough-man government, an attempt to shame the accusing crowd into releasing him? Where he is scourged and crowned and dressed in imperial purple, and whose appearance has less impact than his silence?

The answer is, of course, that it is all four. Bosch has taken elements from all four Gospel accounts and incorporated them into a single painting. This single moment, daubed in oil on wood, becomes every moment. It is Jesus's Passion, once and for all time, and each one of us, every one of us, is caught up in it.

When we look at Bosch's painting we see that to be human is to be political: to be fully human means living in connection with all other human beings, unavoidably involved with social networks and power relationships. To be fully human is to acknowledge that, in some small way, we are *Homo politicus*, people of the city, of the commonwealth of humanity. We live in a political world, as both Bosch and Dylan tell us. We cannot escape that. We live in a world in which violence rules, and injustice is rewarded and the temptation to join in with the violence and injustice is almost overwhelming. But we also live in a world in which Christ was crucified and, because of that fact, the world which crucified him will never be the same again. Love has taken the burden of violence and fear and naked power upon himself, and has redeemed them, transforming them into their holy opposites: compassion and love and willing service. Step into this circle of politics, the painting says to us, but don't be limited by its fearful forces, for as you step through this circle you will encounter Jesus.

Notes

1 Michael Portillo, 'If God is talking to you, too, Mr Cameron – don't listen', *The Sunday Times*, 25 February, 2007.

2 Through this book I will refer to the landscape in which Bosch lived as the 'Lowlands'. This is to avoid the misunderstanding that might come if I talk about 'Holland' (Bosch didn't live in the province of Holland), the 'Netherlands' (which in Bosch's day wasn't the same political entity as the modern day Netherlands), the 'Low Countries' (countries might imply a centralized political structure, which certainly wasn't the case in 1500) or even 'Benelux' (does anyone still use that abbreviation?). For reference, 'Lowlands' means the low-lying principalities, duchies, dioceses and independent cities in the lands drained by the Rhine, Waal and Scheldt rivers, in which, today, you might find beer, lace and chocolate.

3 Richard Foster and Pamela Tudor-Craig, *The Secret Life of Paintings* (Woodbridge: Boydell Press, 1986), p. 5. For the debt of the Lowland painters to the techniques and styles of illuminated manuscripts, see the whole of the very interesting chapter on van Eyck (Chapter 2).

4 *The Image of Christ*, the catalogue of the 'Seeing Salvation' exhibition at the National Gallery, reproduces an English woodcut print from about 1500, in which the dead Christ is shown surrounded by a border of 22 objects and people associated with the Passion: a mocking soldier, the high priest, Peter's cockerel, the lantern of the Temple guards, as well as the dice of the soldiers, the hand that slapped Jesus at the high priest's house and the ladder used to nail the title above Christ's head. *The Image of Pity*, about 1500, in *The Image of Christ* (London: The National Gallery, 2000), pp. 154–5.

5 See Gertrud Schiller, *The Iconography of Christian Art* (London: Lund Humphries, 1971–2), Vol. 2. An example is printed in Foster and Tudor-Craig, *Secret*, p. 62.

6 Dating of the wood upon which the picture is painted shows that it was made, at the earliest, after 1527, after Bosch's death. The most likely attribution is now to Quinten Metsys, a Dutch painter who specialized in copying earlier Dutch masters, so perhaps it is a copy of

another Bosch painting? See Laurinda S. Dixon, *Bosch: Art & Ideas Series* (London: Phaidon, 2003), p. 315.

7 'Political World' on *Oh Mercy* (Columbia Records, CK 45281, 1989).

8 See 'Oak' in James Hall, *Dictionary of Subjects and Symbols in Art* (London: J. Murray, 1974), p. 227.

9 Quoted in Hans Kühner, 'Julius II', Encyclopaedia Britannica Online, www.britannica.com/eb/article-253988 and Norman Davies, *Europe: A history* (Oxford: OUP, 1996) p. 484. Incidentally, Rex Harrison played the role of Julius II in *The Agony and the Ecstasy* (1965) based upon Irving Stone's novel of the life of Michelangelo. Quite the wrong actor for the part: Henry Higgins was far too nice a man to be a Renaissance pope.

10 Michelangelo Buonarroti, *Sonnet 4*, from *Sonnets: The Italian text with an English translation and introduction*, edited and translated by John Addington Symonds (London: Vision Press, 1958). In this edition the sonnet has the title 'On Rome in the Pontificate of Julius II', not Michelangelo's original.

11 The reason it is hackneyed is that whereas once it meant standing up to those people and institutions who could directly and physically harm you (as happened to Martin Luther King in Selma in 1965), now it merely means saying something irritating and self-righteous to those with whom you disagree. It is an expression of the 'victim culture' of our day: Monty Python pinned it neatly with the 'don't you oppress me' sequence in *The Life of Brian* (1979).

12 All biblical quotations are taken from the *New Revised Standard Version (Anglicised edition)*, copyright 1989, 1995 by the Division of Christian Education of the National Council of the Churches of Christ in the United States of America.

13 In Johann Georg Theodor Grässe, *Sagenbuch des Preußischen Staats*, Vol. 1 (Glogau: Verlag von Carl Flemming, 1868), no. 339, p. 301. Available online from *Anti-Semitic Legends*, translated by D. L. Ashliman of the University of Pittsburgh, www.pitt.edu/~dash/anti-semitic.html (accessed 6 April 2008).

14 The Book of Hours of Jean Poyet (or Poyer) is now in the Pierpont Morgan Library in New York (MS H.8), and can be seen in an online exhibition at www.themorgan.org/collections/swf/exhibOnline.asp?id=331 (accessed 6 April 2008). The Mass of St Gregory is folio 168.

15 Diarmaid MacCulloch, *Reformation: Europe's House Divided, 1490–1700* (London: Allen Lane, 2003), pp. 56, 57.

16 Rowan Williams, Sermon to the General Synod of the Church of

England, York Minster, Sunday 9 July 2006. Available online from www.archbishopofcanterbury.org/665 (accessed 6 April 2008).

17 Rowan Williams, 'The End of War', in *South Atlantic Quarterly: Dissent from the Homeland: Essays after September 11*, Vol. 101/2, Spring 2002, p. 271. Walter Wink's exploration of this passage is in his book *Engaging the Powers: discernment and resistance in a world of domination* (Philadelphia: Fortress Press, 1992), Chapter 9, pp. 189–92.

18 We look at these differences between the Gospel accounts in more detail in Circle 5, below.

Circle 2: Elements

Walk into a bookshop and look at the non-fiction shelves. If your shop is anything like my local Waterstone's you will find floor-to-ceiling shelves for what is called 'Mind/Body/Spirit'; if you are lucky, you will find 'Christianity' making do with a half-height shelf, appropriately next to 'Indoor Games'. In the basement the shelves for 'Popular Science' are groaning with such titles as *Why Do Buses Come in Threes?*, *The Hidden Mathematics of Everyday Life*, *What We Believe But Cannot Prove*, *Why Don't Penguins' Feet Freeze?* and *The God Delusion*. The shelves of Waterstone's prove, in a particularly concrete way, that in our day science and religion have nothing to do with one another; to be religious, to be a Christian is, by definition, to *not* believe in science, 'Darwin, evolution and all that'.

We know this to be so because religion and science do not mix: they have nothing to do with one another. We know the history of the rise of science, and we know the part played by religion in general and Christianity in particular in attempting to crush it. The history goes as follows.

The Greeks and the Romans had enquiring minds. Through philosophers, like Plato and Democritus, engineers like Archimedes, astronomers like Ptolemy, and doctors like Galen, they examined the world around them, and described what they found, without the need for interference by the 'gods'. However, for political and morally suspect reasons the Roman Empire succumbed to Christianity, and, with the increase of the power of the Church in the 'dark ages' science and free-thinking was ruthlessly stamped out. Some hints of learning began to re-emerge with the discovery of ancient Greek texts in the Arab world (where learning had never been destroyed) but as soon as the Church realized the implications of this ancient learning (for its teachings about the universe and its own power), it unleashed the full force of the Inquisition on unfortunates like Nicolas Copernicus and Galileo Galilei. As a result, science was once more suppressed in the parts of Europe controlled by the Catholic Church, and it was only because the Protestant churches in northern Europe were weakened by secular authorities that scientific enquiry could continue. Not without a fight, which was only finally won by Darwin's courageous publication of *On the Origin of Species* in 1859. He provided the final nail hammered into the coffin of superstition and faith. Since then, all thinking people have been unbelievers, and anybody who works as a scientist, and yet believes in a religious understanding of the universe actually belongs to the 'Neville Chamberlain' school of science, working for the appeasement of a force that is absolutely and categorically opposed to science.[1] As William Lecky, the rationalist historian wrote in the 1860s:

> It is indeed, marvellous that science should ever have revived amid the fearful obstacles theologians cast in her way. Together with a system of biblical interpretation so stringent, and at the same time so capricious, that it infallibly came into collision with every discovery that was not in accordance with the unaided judgement of the senses, and therefore with the familiar expressions of the Jewish writers, everything was done to cultivate a habit of thought the direct opposite of the habits of science. The constant exaltation of blind faith, the countless miracles, the childish legends, all produced a

condition of besotted ignorance, of grovelling and trembling credulity that can scarcely be paralleled except among the most degraded barbarians.[2]

Reason, and its handmaiden, Science, have had to fight constantly for their existence; even now the forces of superstition seek to destroy their hard-won gains. If we want to see the destructive power of religion, and the reason why it should be eliminated from human civilization, then we just look at the skyline of New York City.

> Imagine, with John Lennon, a world with no religion. Imagine no suicide bombers, no 9/11, no 7/7, no Crusades, no witch-hunts, no Gunpowder plot, no Indian partition, no Israeli/Palestinian wars, no Serb/Croat/Muslim massacres, no persecution of the Jews as 'Christ-killers', no Northern Ireland 'troubles' . . . [*and so on*].[3]

The curious thing is that this belief, common, widespread, unquestioned, is a myth. And not a 'myth' in the sophisticated, philosophical sense of a narrative designed to give coherence and meaning to a person's or a people's experience of life (past and present) and their place in any existing pattern of meaning in the fact of the cosmos. No, the history of the conflict between Christianity and science is a 'myth' in the sense of a 'made-up story'. This made-up story has been incredibly powerful in our culture for almost three hundred years now and, although it has been recognized as such by some scholars for almost a hundred years, it still continues.

This presents us with a problem when we try to understand the next circle in our painting. For Bosch, and for our next circle, there is no such thing as the warfare of religion and science; there is no antagonism between theology and reason. In fact, in order to understand an important component of

Bosch's thinking, and to understand what that means for being a complete human being today, we need to step across the gulf that has been set between theology and science in our own time. It is a difficult thing to do, because it is so much a part of the background to our times and culture: it is a given, unquestioned and unquestionable.

The gulf was first dug, in its popular, twentieth-century form, by two men of whom you've probably never heard: John Draper (1811–82) and Andrew White (1832–1918). Draper, a physician and chemist, and White, an historian and educationalist, wrote two books, hugely influential in their day and subsequently, which are the (unsourced) origins of many of the most cherished stories of the Science-Religion myth.[4] Columbus discovering the world was round, and opposed by theologians? Draper. The excommunication of Halley's comet by Pope Callixtus III in 1456 (cited by astronomers Carl Sagan and Patrick Moore)? Draper again. The refusal by the Church to allow the use of anaesthesia in child-birth? Invented by Andrew White.

We can see how the myth works if we look at one of its seminal events, the public debate surrounding the publication of *On the Origin of Species* in 1859;[5] Draper himself even has a small walk-on part. The 'Myth' tells us that Darwin's ideas, recently and sensationally published, were victorious in a debate held between T. H. Huxley and the Bishop of Oxford, Samuel Wilberforce. The debate followed the presentation of a paper by Draper to the British Association for the Advancement of Science conference in Oxford, June 1860. During the debate, so the story goes, the Bishop, 'Soapy Sam', sarcastically asked Huxley whether he preferred to be descended from an ape on his grandfather's or his grandmother's side. Huxley crushingly replied that 'I would rather be descended from an ape than a bishop', followed by the collapse of the Bishop and the Church party and the triumph of Darwinism: 'Wilberforce was annihilated by Huxley and Hooker, and Darwin's views on evolution started their conquest of the world.'[6]

The reality was that this version of the story is largely based on a gossipy account published (under the title 'A Grandmother's tales') in *Macmillan's Magazine* in October 1898, almost 40 years after the event! The closest thing we have to a participant's account is a letter that Huxley wrote in September 1860:

> If then, said I, the question is put to me would I rather have a miserable ape for a grandfather or a man highly endowed by nature and possessed of great means and influence and yet who employs those faculties for the mere purpose of introducing ridicule into a grave scientific discussion — I unhesitatingly affirm my preference for the ape . . .[7]

Not nearly as catchy as the traditional quip. A neutral observer, *The Athenaeum*, reported the week after the debate that Wilberforce and Huxley 'have each found foemen worthy of their steel, and made their charges and countercharges very much of their own satisfaction and the delight of their respective friends'.[8]

Wilberforce was no scientific ignoramus either.[9] He was vice-president of the BAAS, his original degree (a first) was in mathematics, and he was a noted naturalist. He had written a review of *Origin of Species* which, as Darwin himself admitted, 'picks out with skill all the most conjectural parts, and brings forward well all the difficulties'. Wilberforce himself thought that he had done the better in the hurly-burly of the debate: 'On Saturday Professor Henslow . . . called on me by name to address the Section on Darwin's theory. So I could not escape and had quite a long fight with Huxley. I think I thoroughly beat him.'[10]

The subsequent history of the debate, which improved with the telling, and became more bitter in the recollection, was directed by seismic shifts within the organization of the Victorian scientific enterprise. Wilberforce was representative of the old way of doing things: the gentleman of independent means, able to indulge an interest in, and with an aptitude for, the natural sciences. Darwin was of similar social standing. Huxley, on the other hand, was dependent upon earning his living as a scientist. When, like Darwin, he returned from an exploratory voyage on the *Rattlesnake*, he found it impossible to secure employment: the university positions were restricted to ordained men. 'He built up a sense of anger that people like him, who were trying to secure a place strictly on merit with no family name or wealth or religious credentials, were excluded.'[11]

Therefore, a more accurate understanding of the Huxley–Wilberforce debate would be to recognize it was a dispute about access to patronage that cut across the generations, embellished with large amounts of after-the-event rhetorical improvement. It was a conflict *within* the discipline of natural philosophy, which only later came to be called 'science', rather than a straightforward battle between science and religion.

Even so, today the Huxley–Wilberforce debate[12] stands as an example of all the ways in which we tell ourselves that science and Christianity are enemies: no true scientist can be religious; no true follower of religion can believe in the discoveries of science. The entrenched position satisfies hardliners of both sides, despite betraying confusion about the differences between the nature of the scientific enterprise and the purposes of religion. To say that one 'believes' in science in the same way that one 'believes' in Jesus Christ is to make what philosophers call a 'category error'. The words are being used in a different way; not better, not worse, just different. I 'believe' in science means that my experience shows the scientific method is able to produce a clear, predictable and testable series of results that can be matched against a wider theory of the physical processes at work in the world. I 'believe' in Jesus Christ means that I have an experience of a relationship to which I ascribe value, and in which I experience value in return. The latter 'belief' is unmeasurable (how many kilojoules of 'value' does Jesus generate?) and the former 'belief' is, properly, valueless. I only value the scientific method because I appreciate the results it gives me: electricity to light my house, medicine to treat my ills, calendars to measure my life. Each form of belief has its own natural habitat: I wouldn't want to confuse one for the other, unless I had some very dysfunctional relationships!

Alister McGrath gives a nice example of the importance of recognizing the natural habitat for vocabulary. When he was working as a research biologist in Oxford in the 1970s he and his colleagues would meet for a coffee every morning at 11.00 a.m. If one asked for the sugar, the others didn't demand to know if he meant lactose, fructose, or the sugar with the chemical structure of a 1,2'-glycoside, otherwise known as sucrose. All of these are a form of sugar, but you wouldn't find lactose or fructose palatable in coffee: in the context of a working break, even in the chemistry labs 'sugar' means the sort which comes in packets from Tate & Lyle. Words mean different things in different contexts.[13]

For one evolutionist, Stephen Jay Gould, this distinctiveness of habitat and meaning is demonstrated by the distinctive areas of operation for science and religion. He suggested that science and religion were NOMA (Non-Overlapping Magisteria). Gould proposed:

> . . . the magisterium [the sphere of authority] of science covers the empirical realm: what is the universe made of (fact) and why does it work this way (theory). The magis-

terium of religion extends over questions of ultimate meaning and moral value. These two magisteria do not overlap, nor do they encompass all inquiry (consider, for example, the magisterium of art and the meaning of beauty). To cite the old clichés, science gets the age of rocks, and religion the rock of ages; science studies how the heavens go, religion how to go to heaven.[14]

You won't be surprised to learn that Richard Dawkins doesn't like this theory, believing it to be 'positively supine'. For Dawkins, even if religion is allotted the sphere of 'why' questions, not all why questions are meaningful. It is possible to have a grammatically correct question that is meaningless: he gives as an example, 'Why are unicorns hollow?'[15] This is patently obtuse. Just because *some* 'why' questions are meaningless, it does not follow that *all* 'why' questions are also without meaning. It is possible to construct nonsensical 'how' questions too, perhaps nonsense questions that would appeal to Dawkins: 'How many angels dance on the head of a pin?' For Dawkins there is, and can only ever be, empirical reality: a SOMA perhaps? (A Single Overarching Magisterium.) The only real knowledge is that which comes from observation and experiment, and this knowledge has to come from *public* observation; in other words, there is no reality to things that you alone can see or hear. Experimental knowledge must be able to be repeated in a predictable way; someone else has to be able to get the same data as you, all things being equal. There are no privileged observers or observatories in empirical reality.

But, as Keith Ward has pointed out, there is one example of human experience which cannot be reduced to empirical reality: dreams. We all dream. Scientists have been able to correlate patterns in people's eye movements and brainwaves to the experience of dreaming. If a sleeping subject is woken up as she shows REM (rapid eye movement) she will be able to say that she was dreaming at that moment. Dreams happen. But are they real? Not according to Dawkins's SOMA. They are not publically observable. I might be able to measure your body's responses in such a way as to know that you are dreaming, but I am entirely dependent upon your description of your dreams:

> You observed your dream, no doubt. But I have to trust you as to what the dream was about. I have no access to it. Even your own observation cannot establish that what you say is true, because you only have your memory to rely on, and we know how unreliable that is.[16]

So, Ward makes a distinction between the two, complementary, authorities of science and religion, between the natural sciences and the humanities. The former is concerned with predictable, experimental, publically observable, knowledge. The latter is concerned with conscious, experiential and personal knowledge. An (inadvertent) example of this distinction was shown in a letter to the *Financial Times* as part of a discussion on the relationship between science and religion. Questions, the writer said, about the ultimate origin of the universe are very difficult, 'but ultimately religion cannot answer them. It can only pretend that it does. Fortunately, it has long given up pretending to answer questions like: how can I heat my house? Why is my grandmother coughing?'[17]

The writer's mistake, the mistake of many SOMA-ists, is to think that these sorts of questions (physics, technology, biology) are the only questions worth asking, and that the scientific method is the only legitimate means to provide an answer. Keith Ward shows the absurdity of this artificial limitation: for the scientific method to be the only valid means of enquiry in any endeavour would require the question 'who won the Battle of Waterloo?' to be answered by an equation, and a person's autobiography could be reduced to '25 million micro-tubules resonated at a certain frequency'.[18]

Bearing this in mind, in the last 30 years scholars began to re-examine the relationship of science and religion. A series of religious scientists (or scientific theologians, if you prefer) looked again at what could be learnt about religious faith, if you applied insights from cosmology, anthropology, philosophy and biology. The reverse was also possible: what did the Christian understanding of a Creator, outside space and time, mean when advances in physics were considered? Two of the most creative of these scholars are John Polkinghorne and the late Arthur Peacocke; their ideas deserve to be much more widely known.

From the work of Polkinghorne and Peacocke it is clear that Draper, White, and others, were not writing a fully accurate history, to say the least. Science and religion are not, *by definition*, opposed to each other, and a religious under-standing of life, *by definition*, does not preclude science as a means of understanding the universe. At the very least, there is a *permissive* relationship between religion and the scientific project.

If we remove from consideration religious fundamentalism (which is best regarded as both a loss of nerve in the face of industrialization, and a failure to maintain sophisticated tradi-tions of biblical interpretation by the Church), Christianity, in the breadth of its catholic tradition, has encouraged learning in all spheres of human activity, for moral, theological and practical reasons. The monasteries and universities (religious foundations all) through the so-called 'Dark Ages' retained, developed and deepened our knowledge of the natural sci-ences. Jean Buridan (1300–1358), rector of the University of Paris, developed a theory of impetus that anticipated Newton's First Law of Motion; Nicole d'Oresme (1325–1382), bishop of Lisieux, used advanced algebra in analytic geometry, developing a solution to the problem of motion through space that predated Galileo's 'solution' to the same problem by 300 years; Nicholas of Cusa (1401–1464), a cardinal no less, worked out mathematically that all observers believe themselves to be stationary in an otherwise turning universe. Cusa also developed the mathematical concepts of the infinitesimal and was the first to use concave lenses to correct myopia.

In all these activities, the 'school-men' followed the precepts of Augustine of Hippo. In his commentary on the book of Genesis, Augustine wrote:

> Usually even a non-Christian knows something about the earth, the heavens, and the other elements of this world, about the motion and orbit of the stars and even their size and relative positions, about the predictable eclipses of the sun and the moon, the cycles of the years and the seasons, about the kinds of animals, shrubs, stones, and so forth, and this knowledge he holds to as being certain from reason and experience. Now, it is a disgraceful and dangerous thing for an infidel to hear a Christian, presumably giving the meaning of Holy Scripture, talking nonsense on these topics; and we should take all means to prevent such an embarrassing situation, in which people show up vast ignorance in a Christian and laugh it to scorn.[19]

So, classical Christianity, at the very least, allowed scientific understanding, the application of human reason upon and observation of the natural environment. Some scholars go further. Rodney Stark, the eminent sociologist of religion at Baylor University, Waco, has argued that Judeo-Christian monotheism was the necessary *prerequisite* for science to happen at all. 'In contrast with the dominant religious and philosophical doctrines in the non-Christian world, Christians developed science because they *believed* it *could* be done, and *should* be done.'[20] In other words, because Christians believed both that there was a Creator, and that the Creator was rational, it necessarily followed that the rational capacities of humankind could investigate the rest of creation. God is reasonable, we are made in God's image, therefore we are reasonable, therefore we are able to examine the remainder of his reasonable creation. Augustine, again, put it this way: 'Heaven forbid that God should hate us by which he made us superior to the animals! Heaven forbid that we should believe in such a way as not to accept or seek reason, since we could not even believe if we did not possess rational souls.'[21]

If so great an authority as Augustine of Hippo argued that Christians should be familiar with the latest knowledge about 'the predictable eclipses of the sun and the moon, the cycles of the years and the seasons, about the kinds of animals, shrubs, stones', then it is no wonder that scholars, in those 'dark, benighted years' between the Roman Empire and the Enlightenment, took him at his word and compiled encyclopaedias of human knowledge and divine reason. Such things existed 500 years before that great work of rationalism and anti-clericalism, the *Encyclopédie* of Voltaire, Rousseau and Diderot.

The most influential of these medieval encyclopaedias was written by Bartholomaeus Anglicus, or Bartholomew the Englishman, who was probably born in the very early years of the thirteenth century. He was a student at the great university in Paris in the 1220s, and while there he joined the Franciscans shortly after the Order's foundation. In 1231 he was sent to Magdeburg and taught at its provincial school, while at the same time assisting in the Franciscan preaching missions throughout Eastern Europe. As part of his teaching he compiled the encyclopaedia for which he remains famous: *De proprietatibus rerum* ('On the nature of things'). It was a hugely influential and popular work. Practically every library founded in the Middle Ages has a copy (the National Library in Paris has 18), and often a copy translated into the local vernacular as well. The library of Canterbury Cathedral possesses two leaves from the English edition, translated by John Trevisa and printed by Wynken de Worde in 1495. Scholars of English literature have noted the extensive use that Shakespeare made of Bartholomaeus's work, so much so as to call *DPR* 'Shakespeare's encyclopaedia'.[22]

Bartholomaeus structured his work very carefully. It was divided into 19 books, covering the range of natural philosophy: medicine, chronology, zoology, geography and so on. The number of divisions is not accidental: it was the 12 signs of the zodiac, plus the seven known planets. Bartholomaeus intended to show by this that the work was universal: everything that the well-educated Franciscan needed to know was covered. Beginning properly *de deo* (on God), and covering the nature of angels and the soul, by the fourth book Bartholomaeus was ready to write *de elementis*, the elements, the basic building blocks of the cosmos.

Bartholomaeus Anglicus was following the most sophisticated and widely accepted scientific theory of his day, based upon the work of the Greek philosopher-scientists. Empedocles (c 490 BC–c 430 BC) was first to describe a cosmos made up of four basic units. All matter was composed of varying amounts of fire, water, earth and air. He called these the four 'roots', but later philosophers, among them Plato, preferred the word *stoicheion* (literally 'syllable') to mean 'element', a syllable being the smallest intelligible unit of a word. Each element had a primary and a secondary characteristic. So, fire is primarily warm and secondarily dry; earth is dry then cool; water is cool then moist; and air is moist and secondarily warm. This showed a connectedness between the elements that could be represented in a diagram, with an element positioned on the vertices, and the characteristics along the sides of a square. The important concept to understand is not the division of the universe into its separate elements, but the connectedness of the elements, and the fuzziness of the boundaries along each shared characteristic.

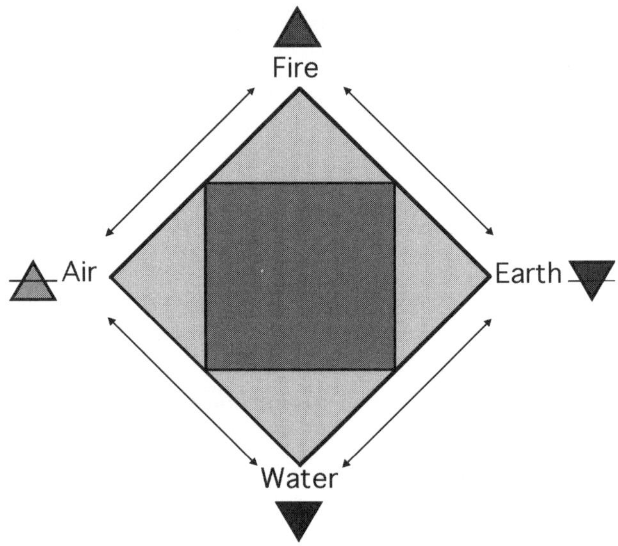

In his dialogue *Timaeus*, Plato described how the elements shared in this geometric relationship:

So god placed water and air between fire and earth, and made them so far as is possible proportional to one another, so that air is to water as water is to earth; and in this way he bound the world into a visible and tangible whole. So by these means and from these four constituents the body of the universe was created to be at unity owing to proportion; in consequence it acquired concord, so that having once come together in unity with itself, it is indissoluble by any but its compounder.[23]

Elements in a proportional relationship could, in theory, be manipulated into changing their qualities. Plato described how each element could transform into another: as all *matter* had been created at the very beginning of time, the different *materials* in the world were the product of the elements transmuting from one form into another. This had implications too for theory of human consciousness: in what way was human identity dependent upon the interaction of these elements? Empedocles himself taught the transmigration of souls, whereby those who, through wickedness, found themselves attached to the matter of the cosmos, were condemned to renew their earthly existence until the divine spark that was their soul could be released from the prison of matter.

The medium for this immortal soul could not be accounted for in the basic theory of the elements, so later philosophers postulated the existence of some fifth element. Plato, in his dialogue *Timaeus*, said that this was 'quintessence' (*quinta essentia*); Aristotle called it *Aether*, and said that it was the material of the heavenly realms. On the earth, existence was subject to decay, and movement was in imperfect straight lines. The heavens had no qualities, for all qualities were subject to decay: they were neither hot, cold, wet, nor dry, and the only change they experienced was change of position, as they moved in their perfect circles. (We shall come across quintessence again, in Circle Five below).

Aristotle's conception of the perfect heavenly realm was an attractive philosophical tool for Christianity, for it made a clear distinction between the corruptibility of human existence ('change and decay in all that I see'), and the perfect nature of God. Bartholomaeus Anglicus showed this application in his compendium:

Of form is diversity, by the which one thing is diverse from another, and some form is essential, and some accidental. Essential form is that which cometh into matter, and maketh it perfect; and accordeth therewith to the perfection of some thing. And when form is had, then the thing hath its being, and when form is destroyed nothing of the substance of the thing is found. And form accidental is not the perfection of things, nor giveth them being. But each form accidental needeth a form substantial. And each form is more simple and more actual and noble than matter. And so the form asketh that shall be printed in the matter, the matter ought to be disposed and also arrayed. For if fire shall be made of matter of earth, it needeth that the matter of earth be made subtle and pured and more simple. Form maketh matter known. Matter is cause that we see things that are made. And so nothing is more common and general than matter.[24]

What Bartholomaeus is saying here, in the admittedly dense English of John Trevisa's fourteenth-century translation, is that things are made up of two qualities: that which is *essential* (of the very essence) and that which is *accidental*. Thus, for example, chairs, whether bought from Ikea or Harrods, share a quality of 'chair-ness', however much they vary in design, colour (or quality!). The accidental form is, by definition, less than perfect, for only in the essential form is perfection to be found ('each form is more simple and more actual and noble than matter'). So we can see how the perfection of heavens (the 'forms') and the imperfection of the world ('matter') are connected: it is an *aspirational* relationship; matter is drawn up towards the perfection of the forms, of which they show merely the imprint of that which is essential.

This theory of the elements had implications for what we would now call physics and chemistry. If there was no creation of matter since the creation of all things by God in the beginning of time, then everything material is related to every other material thing through some combination of the four elements. It should then be theoretically possible to manipulate the elemental constituents of each material so as to make new, different materials. It should be possible to produce, say, gold from lead. Thus the science of alchemy grew out of Platonic and Aristotelian philosophy.

Late medieval alchemy was never the base and corrupt practice that later post-Enlightenment writers made out. Alchemy and alchemists were not just interested in the fortunes that could be made; their primary purpose was to comprehend the processes involved in God's creation. Alchemy's reputation in the modern world has been distorted, Laurinda Dixon argues, by seeing it through the lens of Rosicrucianism. This movement, first mentioned in the early seventeenth century, drew on occult texts from Egypt and a Gnostic understanding of the cosmos; that is, matter is evil and corrupted, and salvation from such corruption is reserved to those who have the secret knowledge (Greek, *gnosis*) handed down to them. This was not the case with alchemy at its zenith in the fifteenth and sixteenth centuries. In Bosch's day

> . . . alchemy was not an occult art, but the practical, legitimate science of distillation, whose laboratory procedures form the basis of modern chemistry. Medieval apothecaries used alchemical apparatus to make artists' paints, women's cosmetics, herbal cooking preparations, and healing potions which they sold in their shops.[25]

The great medieval scientist-friar Roger Bacon (c 1214–94) described the purposes of alchemy as 'a science teaching how to make and procure a certain medicine, called the 'Elixir' which being thrown upon metals, or imperfect bodies, reduces them to absolute perfection'.[26]

This search for perfection was expressed using two Greek concepts. The 'microcosm' of the individual human body would be subsumed into the perfection of the 'macrocosm', the whole created order. 'The transmutation from flawed (sick) to perfect (healed) was accomplished by prayer, study, and physical suffering in imitation of the Passion of Christ, by whose example success could be attained.'[27] Properly, therefore, this was a task of the Church, for whom human salvation was the be-all and end-all, and so alchemy and alchemical investigations were encouraged by all sections of Church and society. Martin Luther said of it:

> . . . rightly and truly the philosophy of the sages of old, with which I am well pleased, not only by reason of its virtue and manifold usefulness . . . but also by reason of the noble and beautiful likeness which it hath with the resurrection of the Dead on the Day of Judgement.[28]

As in the earth below, so too in the heavens above. From the earliest years of human observation it was seen that the sun followed a repeated path in the sky: later astronomers called this the ecliptic. Behind the sun were constellations of fixed stars and, following behind the sun, sometimes above and sometimes below, moved a much smaller number of wandering stars, the planets. An explanation for these observations was needed, and the medieval world turned to philosopher-theologians for the answer.

The philosopher-theologians based their ideas upon the work of our old friend Aristotle, and in particular his two treatises, *On the Heavens* and *Metaphysics*. A monumental series of commentaries were written on these two works, the most influential of which was Peter Lombard's (c 1095–1160) *Sententiae* ('Sentences' or 'Opinions'), which became the standard theological textbook for the next 400 years. Lombard wrote in a question-and-answer style, and such was his influence that this was adopted as the standard format for cosmology: Peter Grant has catalogued over 400 different works (up to the seventeenth century) which were arranged around such questions as 'whether the universe is eternal'; 'what is creation?'; 'how many fixed stars are there?'[29]

Among the philosopher-theologians there was a fundamental agreement in the structure of the cosmos. First, the cosmos was a unique, *finite* sphere. Second, following Aristotle, it was thought that the cosmos was divided into two parts. The 'celestial' or 'translunary' region began at the orbit of the moon and reached to the outermost part of the cosmos, at least as far as the fixed stars, and even beyond. The 'sublunar', or 'terrestrial' region began again at the orbit of the moon, and extended down to the earth's core, which was assumed to be the geometric centre of the universe.

The earth's position at the centre of the universe is often thought today to indicate an unwarranted self-importance in medieval cosmology: to think of oneself as being at the centre of the universe is a sign of overweening pride; medieval man was similarly conceited. But, as we shall see, there was actually no confusing geometric centrality with ethical centrality: in other words, the fact that the earth was at the centre of the heavens was an indication of the earth's imperfections and unimportance.

Don't believe polemicists who say that medieval man thought the earth was flat: he knew that it was neither flat nor a sphere. As Pierre d'Ailly (1350–1420) put it:

> . . . although there are mountains and valleys on the earth, for which reason it is not perfectly round, it approximates very nearly to roundness. Thus it is that an eclipse of the moon, which is caused by the shadow of the earth, appears round. They say the earth is round, therefore, because it approximates to roundness.[30]

There was a theological as well as an empirical reason why the earth could not be a perfect sphere. It was believed that the sublunar region (from the earth to the moon) was a place of continual change and decay:

> Above the variable sky there were the heavenly bodies which seemed to have been perfectly regular in their behaviour ever since the first observations were made and of which none, to his [i.e. medieval man's] knowledge, had ever been seen to come into existence or to decay. The Moon was obviously the lowest of these. Hence he divided the universe at the Moon; all above that was necessary, regular and eternal, all below it, contingent, irregular and perishable.[31]

The earth below was subject to change (which meant decay). The heavens above were not subject to decay so, according to Aristotle, the only change that can occur in the heavens is change of place or position: empirical observation, after all, shows us that the planets and stars changed position. Their movement was explained by the theory that they were embedded in invisible orbs or spheres which themselves were moved, and many of the questions and answers in the cosmologies concentrated on the means by which the spheres were moved and how they were arranged: there were two major theories.

Those who followed Aristotle assumed 55 concentric spheres, commonly centred on the geometric centre of the earth and cosmos.[32] Some of these spheres were 'rolling' and others 'unrolling' spheres, with 33 of them assigned to the movement of the planets alone. Aristotle's explanation is as obscure as it is brief, and so it is understandable that a rival explanation was constructed to explain the observable evidence. This was the work of the Greco-Egyptian astronomer Claudius Ptolemaeus (c AD 100 – c AD 170), more commonly known as Ptolemy. For

Ptolemy, the planets were fixed upon spheres which followed both eccentric and epicyclic paths; that is, the centre of the sphere was not fixed at the centre of the earth and so, in certain passages around the sphere, the planet or the sun would appear to be moving faster away from earth than at other points on the orbit. An epicyclic motion meant that as each planet revolved around the earth on its large, grand sphere (the deferent), it was *also* revolving on a smaller cycle, the epicycle. This explained why, on some days of the year, the planets' orbit appeared to slow down or even regress.[33]

Simply (and thus, crudely), we can say that if the medieval natural philosopher had been able to travel in space he would have crossed spheres in this order: the moon, Mercury, Venus, the sun, Mars, Jupiter, and Saturn. Beyond the seventh sphere was that of the fixed stars, the *stellatum*. This was not thought to be close to the earth. For example, *The South English Legendary*, a collection of poems about the saints in an artless English of the thirteenth century later arranged into the calendar of the Church's year, showed exactly how large this poky universe was thought to be:

> Much is between heaven and earth • for the man that
>   might go
> Every day forty miles • ever upwards and even more
> He should not to the highest heaven • that you everyday
>   seeth
> Come in eight thousand years • there as the stars be.[34]

That's 116,880,000 miles, in a world in which 40 miles was more than a full day's journey. To the medieval mind, the universe was vast, and grand and complex, and humanity, on our small earth, was (spatially) insignificant.

The final sphere was the *Primum Mobile*, 'the first mover'. It was called that because beyond it was the immobile sphere, the empyrean or heaven. According to Anselm of Laon (d. 1117), the empyrean was 'fiery or intellectual, which is so called not by virtue of its burning but from its brilliance, since it is immediately filled with angels'.[35] The empyrean had to be immobile, for it is the sphere of the blessed dead, who are in the state of perfect rest: Greek philosophy meets Christian theology.

> In medieval science the fundamental concept was that of certain sympathies, antipathies, and strivings inherent in matter itself. Everything has its right place, its home, the region that suits it, and, if not forcibly restrained, moves thither by a sort of homing instinct.[36]

This is what Chaucer called the 'kyndely enclyning'[37] of inanimate creation. Everything, within the terrestrial sphere, tended to its rightful place, and through that tendency, all matter was transmutable, and all matter was interconnected in its very essence. The three groups of celestial objects – constellations, planets and sun – combined to influence human affairs on the earth below (more accurately, as we have seen, the earth *within*). This influence was systematized in the exceedingly complicated belief system that was renaissance astrology.

Astrology was more than just prediction, just as biblical prophecy was more than just foretelling God's actions. In its richest forms it was a system of structuring knowledge about the full breadth of human society and its relationship with the created order: it covered what we would now understand as sociology, political science, meteorology, psychology as well as astronomy and speculative cosmology. We shouldn't think that men studied astrology because they were foolish or superstitious or credulous. They studied astrology because they wanted to understand the world in which they lived and the times and culture in which they found themselves. C. S. Lewis puts it this way: 'Astrology was a hard-headed, stern, anti-idealistic affair; the creed of men who wanted a universe which admitted no incalculables. Magic sought power over nature; astrology proclaimed nature's power over man.'[38]

An example of the richness and complexity of this world view is found in the *Très Riches Heures du Duc de Berry*, produced for Jean, Duc de Berry between 1412 and 1416 by three brothers, Herman, Paul, and Johan Limbourg, from Nijmegen in the Dutch Lowlands.[39] Along with scenes of the changing activities over the course of the calendar year, it includes richly illuminated paintings of the life of Christ, an imaginative aerial view of Rome, and an anatomical man, surrounded by the signs of the zodiac displayed in the painting's border (folio 14v).[40] Each sign of the zodiac was assigned to one of the elements in four groups called 'triplicities': the Fire signs were Aries, Leo, Sagittarius; the Water signs were Cancer, Scorpio, Pisces, and so on. So we see in the top left-hand corner Aries, the ram, and March, the month of Mars is above the Zodiacal Man's right shoulder.[41] Aries is the first sign, and March, at this time, the first month of the year. Astrologers taught that the 'domicile' of Aries was the planet Mars (when Mars is in the 'domicile' of Aries, in the same part of the night sky as the constellation, the influence of Mars upon the world, and especially people born under the sign of Aries, is that much greater). Aries is also one of the 'Fire signs' of the zodiac, all three of which share common qualities of vigorousness and new beginnings. Men with this horoscope were thought to be confident, assertive, full of energy and aggression. The ambitious man would be under the sign of Mars, and he would succeed through force of will. It was the sign of the soldier.

Above Zodiacal Man's left shoulder is Aquarius. Despite being the water-bearer, Aquarius is one of the three Air signs. In some astrological schemes, the Air signs are ruled by

Saturn, but in others Jupiter is their house, the god of thunderstorms and lightning.[42] Jupiter, in his Greek form Zeus, was first worshipped as an oracle in the oak groves of Dodona: the oak tree was sacred to Jupiter and so the god was often depicted wearing a wreath of oak leaves.[43] Air was thought to be the universal power (look at the biblical importance placed upon the breath of God), and so those ruled by the Air signs were creative powers: the future and ideas were all subject to the influence of Air. It was the sign of the thinker, but perhaps a cold and calculating one.

One sign below Aquarius is Capricorn, an 'Earth' sign, whose ruling planet was Saturn. Saturn was the god of the earth, and all its fruitfulness. But Saturn's roots were in the ancient Greek god Cronos, famous for his cruelty (he castrated his father and ate his children). Therefore Saturn was a 'maleficent sign',[44] and was known as the Greater Infortune, *Infortuna Major*.

The Earth signs controlled characteristics like hard work, pragmatism and diligence, although those born under Capricorn could tip over into a dull materialism. They were dark of appearance and nature. It was the sign of the merchant.

By Zodiacal Man's left hand is Cancer, the crab. Cancer was one of the 'Water' signs, whose members were prone to sensitivity, emotion and a strong connection to the past. Cancer is controlled by the moon, with all the dangers of instability that implies: the close connection between Luna and lunacy should remind us of that.

We have spent much time and effort in trying to recover the late medieval understanding of the connection between religion and science, to describe the assumptions held by the learned scholar of both scripture and nature in Bosch's day. We have seen that the world view of the late Middle Ages had at its base the Platonic/Aristotelian theory of 'elemental science'; all matter was made up of various combinations of four basic building blocks: fire, water, air and earth. Aristotle postulated the existence of a further element, quintessence, which was useful in explaining the perfection of the heavens compared with the corruption of the earth. We have seen how elemental science depended upon the religious use of reason: belief in a reasonable God allowed scholars to examine His reasonable creation using the gift of human reason. We have seen how some churchmen systematized this reasonable project in great compendia and encyclopaedia, hundreds of years before the Enlightenment gave us the very word. We have seen how elemental science was worked out in the material sciences (in the form of alchemy), and cosmology (in the form of astrology). We will also see, in the next circle, the implications for biology and the psychological sciences, in the form of humoral and temperamental medicine. We have also seen how elemental science was expressed in the practical and artistic artefacts of the period, in the Barber Surgeons' handbook and the *Book of Hours of the Duc de Berry*. What about Bosch? Are we now in a place to see the way in which *Christ Mocked* also shares in this world view?

Bosch ascribed a *political* role to each of the four tormentors. Now, subtly, he also ascribes an *elemental* role, that builds upon, but is not completely identified with, each tormentor's political role. Let us look at them in turn.

The green man, we have seen, stands for the secular powers of Europe. But, following the Zodiacal Man, he takes the position of elemental Fire, ruled by Mars, the god of war. In Zodiacal Man it was believed that the constellation of Aries controlled the cranium and the jaw, the voluntary impulses of a person. And so we can see the green man, with his jaw clenched, poised in the moment before he rams the crown of thorns onto Christ's head. Action is being taken, a moment is being forced to its crisis, and Fire is the instigator.

In the politics circle the dark man stood for the power of

the Church, and its part in the persecution of the body of Christ. In this circle of Elements he stands in the position for Air, and its ruling planet of Jupiter. Notice how he wears a sprig of oak in his hat, a symbol of the Roman god. Look too at the cold, calculating look on his face. He is not the man to inflict pain upon Christ; rather, he is the man who has the bright idea that this troublemaker needs to be got rid of: he makes the nails for others to hammer.

The man in rose is in the place of the elemental Earth and the Earth signs symbolized by Capricorn. His features are dark and heavy and he is slipping away from the rest of the group, into the darkness beyond the corner of the picture. His clothes are plain but expensive: a subtle rose-coloured robe and a dark hood. Is he a merchant? One who knows the value of the business that Christ can bring, and so stretches out to grasp onto his 'sure thing'. The two-handed grasp reminds me of the Sufi tale of the monkey and the bottle: the best way to catch a monkey is to put cherries inside a glass bottle. The monkey will grasp the cherries and its clenched fist will then be too wide to remove from the bottle's neck. The monkey is trapped, by its greed, until the hunter comes to kill him. The man in rose is so intent on keeping hold of his business investment that he is unable to prevent his steady slide out of the picture.

The old man has a watery face, with brimming eyes and a dripping nose. He is elemental Water, and he is ruled by the moon, which even appears on his headdress. There is something disconnected about his gaze, and his hands are placed in an uncomfortable manner on Christ's lap. Is there a slipperiness, a mutability, about his demeanour that seems like the heaviness of water?

What does this interpretation add to our understanding of the picture? The answer comes from comprehending how Bosch has arranged his four elemental tormentors. They are crowded around Christ, surrounding him on every side, but not in a gentle or dependent manner. The one through whom all things were made, the one upon whom all creation is dependent for its very being, is being threatened by his own creation. Creation has turned on Creator. Hands that flung stars into space are now tormented by the very material he created. This is not the mocking of one man, Bosch is saying. This is a battle that is fought on cosmic lines, that involves everything that ever was and everything that ever will be.

In this respect, Bosch is absolutely orthodox in his presentation of Christian teaching. In his composition there must be a memory of or a reference to the Letter to the Colossians. In that letter Paul warns his congregation against the dangers of being taken in by false teaching: 'See to it that no one takes you captive through philosophy and empty deceit, according to human tradition, according to the elemental spirits of the universe, and not according to Christ.' (Colossians 2.8)

The textual notes to the *New Revised Standard Version* point out that 'elemental spirits' could also be translated as 'rudiments of the world'. This is the translation preferred by Walter Wink, in his seminal series on the powers of the New Testament. Wink argues that 'elements' here means 'the first or fundamental principles of the physical universe'. They are not just patterns derived from human thinking:

> They are given within nature, patterned into organisms and objectified in science, symbols, images, art, rules and religions. These function in nature and society the way electrostatic bonds function in molecules: they operate to hold the shape or maintain the stability of physical, biological and cultural systems.[45]

Wink prefers to call these elements 'invariances'. He points out that although Greek philosophers might have treated them as divine, this did not mean that they were personal, in the sense that Christians believe that God is personal. Their divinity came from ultimacy: it was not possible to conceive of anything more basic than these elements, invariances. But Paul asserted an invariant which preceded the invariances of Greek philosophy:

> He is the image of the invisible God, the firstborn of all creation; for in him all things in heaven and on earth were created, things visible and invisible, whether thrones or dominions or rulers or powers — all things have been created through him and for him. (Colossians 1.15–16)

All elements were created through him and for him, and yet, here in his Passion and in the mocking, Bosch shows us how the elements have turned on their Creator.

So what can we take away from this Circle of the Elements? Let us set aside for one moment the truth, or otherwise, of Bosch's scientific understanding of the cosmos (in the narrow sense of truth demanded by Dawkins's SOMA). Elemental and astrological understandings of nature have been super-seded by chemistry and astronomy (although the assumptions of Newtonian physics on the micro- and macro-scales are, apparently, being overturned by quantum mechanics).[46] We should instead take to heart the fact that Bosch thought it entirely appropriate, in a devotional work of art, to depict the most sophisticated scientific understanding of his day. There was nothing wrong with him referencing science in a 'religious' painting. He would not understand Stephen Jay Gould's thesis that science and religion are NOMAs. For Bosch, we can infer that in order to understand the Creator it was necessary for him to understand the creation; in order to worship the Creator, it was necessary for the faithful artist to represent (re-present) the Creator's creation back to him.

The universe in which Bosch lived does not have a high

regard in the eyes of some empirical realists of our day. Richard Dawkins says this:

> The universe is genuinely mysterious, grand, beautiful, awe-inspiring. The kinds of views of the universe which religious people have traditionally embraced have been puny, pathetic, and measly in comparison to the way the universe actually is. The universe presented by organised religions is a poky little medieval universe, and extremely limited.[47]

This is no more than assertive ignorance: the 'poky little medieval universe' inhabited by Bosch was none of those things. It was a cosmos of incomparable complexity and richness, in which all parts of creation were affected by and acted upon by all other parts, in which humanity, although sharing in a fallen and degraded position in the world, was still able to comprehend and represent the cosmos. Think of *St John the Evangelist on Patmos*, and the woodcuts by Michael Wolgemut of the creation of the world in *The Nuremberg World Chronicle* (1493).[48] Is this a poky little universe? It might be criticized for its failings on empirical grounds, but can it be faulted aesthetically?

We have a better understanding of the world inhabited by Bosch now, and his integration of a scientific understanding and a confessional understanding of the cosmos. This becomes a challenge for us in our own day and culture. Where are the great art works of today which show such a familiarity with scientific understandings? The Wellcome Collection seems to be the only gallery in London which sets out to explore the relationship between science, medicine and the arts. Where are the paintings and sculptures and musical works in our churches which show this wholly integrated understanding of humanity as reasonable creatures in God's reasonable creation? I know of two stained-glass windows made in the last 30 years in Durham Cathedral.

One, paid for by Marks and Spencer, shows an abstract representation of the Last Supper, depicting the 'Divine Economy'[49] at work and its part to play in the economy of human relationships. It is a fine and moving work of art, but even though economics is often called the 'dismal science' by its detractors, isn't it a branch of the humanities rather than an empirical science? Another window in the south quire aisle depicts technology and industry in the north-east. It is stilted and cartoon-like, with a toy-town colliery winding wheels.[50] It is not a great work of art, and it portrays industrialization, rather than any philosophy of the scientific method. The National Cathedral in Washington DC famously has a window that commemorates 'Scientists and Technicians', and contains a particle of moon rock donated by the Apollo 11 astronauts. The artist, Rodney Winfield, deliberately set out to evoke the 'macrocosm and microcosm of space'. There is something of the wonder of modern cosmology here, and Bosch would have understood the artist's religious intentions as well, but it is a rare example.

What of popular music? Vangelis, the Greek composer most famous for his film score for *Chariots of Fire*, released an album in the early 1970s called *Albedo 0.39* after the measurement of light reflection from the earth back into space. The nine pieces of music are all inspired by astronomical science, with titles like 'Pulstar', 'Mare tranquilitatis' and 'Sword of Orion'. Brian Eno is another musician, working in the strange gap between rock, the avant garde and classical forms, who tries to take science seriously: '. . . for years (since my teens) I've been fascinated by the conversation that's been going on in the sciences – particularly the life sciences and the commuter [sic] sciences'.[51]

In 1978 he even produced a record called *Before and After Science*. In his review for *Rolling Stone*, Tom Carson said: 'Brian Eno's position is ambiguous almost by definition: a perfect child of science, he uses its rationalism to celebrate mystery.

For him, technology is not bloodless machinery, but a wondrous instrument of delight.'[52]

We can see from our painting that Bosch shared in that delight. However, in our day, signs of a fruitful and open conversation between the arts and sciences (and especially religious art and science) are few and far between. Have we really progressed at all from Bosch's day, and his desire to participate in the great conversation of reason? In this instance, Richard Dawkins is right. The universe is genuinely mysterious, grand, beautiful and awe-inspiring. As we gaze upon Bosch's depiction of that mysterious horror and beauty we should remind ourselves to search for awe in every part of our lives. If we are able to do that, then we will recognize with Bosch and with Gerard Manley Hopkins:[53]

> The world is charged with the grandeur of God.
> It will flame out, like shining from shook foil;
> It gathers to a greatness, like the ooze of oil
> Crushed. Why do men then now not reck his rod?
> Generations have trod, have trod, have trod;
> And all is seared with trade; bleared, smeared with toil;
> And wears man's smudge and shares man's smell: the soil
> Is bare now, nor can foot feel, being shod.
> And for all this, nature is never spent;
> There lives the dearest freshness deep down things;
> And though the last lights off the black West went
> Oh, morning, at the brown brink eastward, springs —
> Because the Holy Ghost over the bent
> World broods with warm breast and with ah! bright wings.

Notes

1 Richard Dawkins's happy phrase in *The God Delusion* (London: Bantam Press, 2006), pp. 66ff.

2 W. E. H. Lecky, *History of the Rise and Influence of the Spirit of Rationalism* (London: Longman, 1865), 2 vols. Vol. 1, pp. 300–1. See also

Philip J. Sampson, *Six Modern Myths about Christianity and Western Civilization* (Downers Grove, IL: IVP, 2001), p. 28. A later, 1910, edition of Lecky's work was published for the Rationalist Press Association.

3 Dawkins, *God Delusion*, p. 1.

4 John W. Draper, *The History of the Conflict between Religion and Science* (1874) and Andrew D. White, *A History of the Warfare of Science with Theology in Christendom* (1896).

5 For an examination of the reality behind the other key episodes in the history of the 'conflict' see Rodney Stark, *For the Glory of God: How monotheism led to reformations, science, witch-hunts, and the end of slavery* (Princeton, NJ; Oxford: Princeton University Press, 2003), especially Chapter 2; Sampson, *Six Modern Myths*; Ian G. Barbour, *Religion and Science: Historical and Contemporary Issues* (London: SCM, 1998). Keith Ward, *Pascal's Fire: Scientific faith and religious understanding* (Oxford: Oneworld, 2006) has a characteristically breezy and engaging discussion of Galileo's troubles.

6 Gavin de Beer, 'Charles Darwin' in Charles Gillispie, ed., *The Dictionary of Scientific Biography* (New York: Scribner's, 1971), Vol. 3, p. 574.

7 Thomas Huxley, quoted in J. Vernon Jensen, 'Return to the Wilberforce–Huxley Debate', *British Journal for the History of Science*, Vol 21 (January 1988), p. 167. See also J. R. Lucas, 'Wilberforce and Huxley: A legendary encounter', *Historical Journal*, Vol. 22/2 (1979), pp. 313–30. (Available online from http://users.ox.ac.uk/~jrlucas/legend.html, accessed 6 April 2008.)

8 Vernon Jensen, 'Return', p. 170.

9 Despite descriptions of him which deprecate his expertise: according to Gavin de Beer, he 'knew little of natural history, but was coached by the anatomist Richard Owen, who was jealous at what he felt already was Darwin's ascendency over himself'. De Beer, 'Darwin', p. 574.

10 Samuel Wilberforce, Letter to Sir Charles Anderson, 3 July 1860, quoted in Keith Stewart Thomson, 'Huxley, Wilberforce and the Oxford Museum' in *American Scientist*, Vol 88/3 (May–June 2000), p. 210. Vernon Jensen notes the rather theatrical way in which the debate was conducted. According to one eyewitness, Wilberforce included in his remarks this playful comment, 'I should like to ask Professor Huxley, who is sitting by me, and is about to tear me to pieces when I have sat down . . .' Vernon Jensen, 'Return', p. 178.

11 Vernon Jensen, 'Return', p. 175. See also Frank M. Turner, 'The Vic-

torian Conflict between Science and Religion: A Professional Dimension' in *Isis*, Vol. 69/3 (Sept. 1978), pp. 356–76.

12 For further discussion on this dispute, see David Lindberg and Ronald Numbers, 'Beyond War and Peace: A Reappraisal of the Encounter between Christianity and Science' in *Perspectives on Science and Christian Faith*, Vol. 39.3, Sept. 1987, pp. 140-9, and Owen Chadwick, *The Secularization of the European Mind in the Nineteenth Century* (Cambridge: CUP, 1975), pp. 161–88.

13 Alister McGrath, *Dawkins' God: Genes, memes and the meaning of life* (Oxford: Blackwell Publishing, 2005), pp. 97f.

14 Stephen Jay Gould, *Rocks of Ages: Science and religion in the fullness of life* (New York: Ballantine, 1999), p. 6. The second of those old clichés is often attributed to Galileo, who was quoting Cesare, Cardinal Baronius (1538–1607), the ecclesiastical historian and Librarian to the Vatican. It was Baronius, in his *Annales Ecclesiastici*, who came up with the unfortunate concept of the 'Dark Ages' for the period between 500 and 1100.

15 Dawkins, *God Delusion*, pp. 55, 56.

16 Keith Ward, *Pascal's Fire*, p. 119. The whole of Chapter 9 is an excellent discussion of the differences between 'reality' and 'value', and how they relate to science and religion.

17 Graham Giller, 'Persistent myth of war between science and religion', Letters to the Editor, *Financial Times*, 11 October 1997, p. 8.

18 Keith Ward, 'Pascal's Fire: Scientific faith and religious understanding', a lecture given at Gresham College, London, 27 June 2006. Available online from www.gresham.ac.uk.

19 Augustine, *De genesi ad litteram* ('The Literal Meaning of Genesis'), 1.19, translated by John Hammond Taylor in *The Literal Meaning of Genesis: Ancient Christian Writers Series*, no. 41 (New York: Newman Press, c 1982), Vol. 1. pp. 42–3.

20 Stark, *For the glory of God*, p. 147. Emphasis in the original.

21 Augustine, Epistle 120 (to Consentius), quoted in David C. Lindberg, 'Science and the Early Christian Church', *Isis*, Vol. 74, No. 4. (December 1983), p. 517. See also David C. Lindberg and Ronald L. Number, eds, *God and nature: Historical essays on the encounter between Christianity and science* (Berkeley, CA; London: University of California Press, 1986), pp. 27–8.

22 See D. C. Greetham, 'The concept of nature in Bartholomaeus Anglicus' in *Journal of the History of Ideas*, Vol. 41, No. 4. (Oct.–Dec. 1980), pp. 663–77.

23 Plato, *Timaeus*, § 32, in Desmond Lee, trans., Penguin Classics (London: Penguin, 1971) pp. 44f.

24 Quoted in Robert Steele (ed.), *Medieval lore from Bartholomew Anglicus* (Whitefish, MT: Kessinger Publishing, 1893/2007), p. 16.

25 Laurinda Dixon, 'Bosch's Garden of Delights Triptych: Remnants of a "Fossil" Science' in *The Art Bulletin*, Vol. 63, No. 1. (March 1981), p. 98. I think Dixon is using the word 'occult' here as a synonym for 'bad magic', in a negative sense. Alchemy certainly was a *mystical* discipline that sought to bring its practitioners privileged knowledge of the universe, and because of this it was occasionally proscribed by the Church. The important point Dixon is making stands: alchemy had practical, beneficial, goals for society. (I am grateful to Dr David Arnott for this and other insights on scientific questions in this chapter.)

26 Roger Bacon, *The Philosopher's Stone*, quoted in Dixon, 'Fossil Science', p. 98.

27 Dixon, 'Fossil Science', p. 98.

28 Quoted in Dixon, 'Fossil Science', p. 98.

29 See Appendix 1: 'Catalogue of Questions' in Edward Grant, *Planets, Stars, and Orbs: The Medieval Cosmos, 1200–1687* (Cambridge; New York: CUP, 1994), pp. 681 seq.

30 Pierre d'Ailly, *The Image of the World*, quoted in Grant, *Planets*, pp. 619–20.

31 C. S. Lewis, *Studies in Medieval and Renaissance literature* (Cambridge: CUP, 1966), p. 42.

32 Aristotle, *Metaphysics*, 12.8.

33 The whole question of Aristotelian versus Ptolemaic cosmology is comprehensively set out in Grant, *Planets*, 'Part II: The Celestial Region', pp. 189 seq.

34 Charlotte D'Evelyn and Anna J. Mill, eds, *The South English legendary* (London: Early English Text Society/OUP, 1956-9). Vol 2. ll. 489-92. My own translation.

35 *Glossia ordinaria*, quoted in Grant, *Planets*, p. 372.

36 C. S. Lewis, *The Discarded Image: An introduction to medieval and renaissance literature* (Cambridge: CUP, 1964/1994), p. 92.

37 'Geffrey, thou wost ryght wel this, / That every kyndely thyng that is / Hath a kyndely stede ther he / May best in hyt conserved be; / Unto which place every thyng / Thorgh his kyndely enclynyng / Moveth for to come to / Whan that hyt is awey therfro' ('Geoffrey, you know well that everything there is in nature has a natural place

where it is best conserved; toward this place everything is naturally inclined and moves to come to that place when it is far away from it'). Chaucer, *Hous of Fame* (c 1380), II. 729-36. It is in this poem that 'galaxy' and 'Milky Way' first appear.

38 C. S. Lewis, *Studies in Medieval and Renaissance literature* (Cambridge: CUP, 1966), p. 56.

39 Now in the Musée Condé, Chantilly (Ms. 65). Displayed online (in French) at www.institut-de-france.fr/animations/berry/berry.swf (accessed 23 October 2007).

40 See the copy on Wikimedia Commons website at http://commons. wikimedia.org/wiki/Image:Anatomical_Man.jpg (accessed 6 April 2008). The Guildbook of the Barber Surgeons of York also shows a Zodiac Man, which makes explicit the connection between parts of the body to the zodiacal signs: Sagittarius, the thighs; Aquarius, the shins; Scorpio, the genitals, and so on! (British Library, MS Egerton 2572 f.50v).

41 A recent book, written from a position of sympathy to the teachings of Western astrology is Neil Spencer, *True as the Stars Above: Adventures in Modern Astrology* (London: Gollancz, 2000), especially Chapter 2. Please bear in mind that the present author does not necessarily sub-scribe to the teachings of modern astrology, and is certainly not advo-cating it as a philosophy of life or a guide to ethical conduct. I am interested in what we can imaginatively reconstruct of the astrological world view of Bosch and his contemporaries.

42 Especially in Western astrology influenced by the astrology of the Near East. Albumasar (Abu Ma'shar), 787-866, assigned Mars to ele-mental fire and humoral yellow bile, and Jupiter to elemental air. Al-Biruni, 973-1048, applied Saturn to elemental earth and black bile humour. Anselm translated the former into Latin in 1100, and the Italian Guido Bonatti referred to the teachings of the latter. See Dorian Gieslar Greenbaum, *Temperament: Astrology's Forgotten Key* (Bournemouth: Wessex Astrologer, 2005), pp. 24-7.

43 See 'Jupiter' in James Hall, *Dictionary of Subjects and Symbols in Art* (London: J. Murray, 1974), p. 182.

44 See Tamsyn Barton, *Ancient Astrology* (London: Routledge, 1994), especially Chapter 4.

45 Walter Wink, *Unmasking the Powers: The invisible forces that determine human existence* (Philadelphia: Fortress Press, 1986) pp. 130, 132.

46 Although your car doesn't move using quantum forces. Yet.

47 Richard Dawkins, 'A Survival Machine' in John Brockman, ed., *The*

Third Culture (New York: Simon & Schuster, 1996), quoted in Alister McGrath, *Dawkins' God: Genes, memes and the meaning of life* (Oxford: Blackwell Publishing, 2005), p. 146.

48 Larry Silver, *Hieronymus Bosch* (New York: Abbeville Press, 2006), p. 179. Wolgemut was the teacher of Albrecht Dürer. See Wikimedia for a reproduction of Wolgemut's creation series, especially the folio 5v, the Seventh Day, http://commons.wikimedia.org/wiki/ Category: Nuremberg_Chronicle.

49 It is actually called 'The Daily Bread window', Mark Angus 1984 (donated by the staff of Marks and Spencer, Durham, to mark the firm's centenary).

50 *Millennium Window*, 1996–1997, by Joseph Nuttgens.

51 'Brian Eno – in conference with CompuServe on July 4th, 1996 at his London studio'. Available online from www.enoweb.co.uk, or at http://music.hyperreal.org/artists/brian_eno/interviews/ciseno.ht ml (accessed 6 April 2008). 'Commuter' is presumably a typo for 'computer'.

52 Tom Carson, untitled review, *Rolling Stone*, 18 May 1978. Available online from http://music.hyperreal.org/artists/brian_eno/inter-views/rs78b.html (accessed 6 April 2008).

53 'God's Grandeur', written in 1877, while training for the priesthood at St Beuno's in North Wales.

Circle 3: Temperaments

Imagine you wish to invent a new religion. You have already decided that in order to spread your message about, say, the great Flying Spaghetti Monster in the Sky[1] your religion will need to have a group of people, with specialized training in the teachings of Spaghettism. The training will not be appropriate for all followers of your religion (takes too long, requires a certain level of educational attainment, is too demanding), but you do not wish to limit your disciples to a certain number or a certain type of person: this is not a secret sect; the Church of the Flying Spaghetti Monster is open to all men and women. Remembering the wise saying that 'it takes all sorts', you set out to recruit all kinds of men and women to be your professional Spaghettists; the 'pastas', if you like. Now, here's the thing: how long do you think it will be before your body of religious professionals resemble each other more than they resemble the breadth of your adherents? Six months? Six years? Never?

This is a question that has been asked recently of the Church of England. In the *Church Times* in March 2007, Leslie Francis, at that time Professor of Practical Theology at the University of Wales in Bangor, published his findings on the personality types of the clergy.[2] A series of studies (some concentrating on the Church in Wales) by Francis and his colleagues examined the personality types of a range of congregations and clergy. In earlier surveys, they had found that both congregations and clergy were preponderantly from the ISFJ section of the Myers-Brigg Type Indicator/Keirsey Temperament Sorter (the grouping characterized as 'introverts, sensers, feelers, and judgers: we shall come to Myers-Brigg and the 'Four Letter Temperaments' in a while). This identical typing may not be a bad thing. When the clergy and their congregations hold similar personality profiles, there may also be a common vision for the Church. ISFJ clergy tend to be good at ministering to ISFJ congregations.[3]

However, this happy match is not always the case. In a further study, Francis surveyed the temperaments of clergy in the Church of England. This revealed that there is a much higher proportion of the 'Intuition' type among clergy than congregations:

A higher proportion of intuitive leaders may shape a Church that is more open to change, theological and liturgical. But a Church in which leaders are seeking change and the members are seeking stability may also experience greater internal conflict.

Francis concluded his article with the perennial rallying cry of the academic: 'further work—further research—is urgent'.[4]

This further research into questions of human personality types is not a new thing. Sometimes you might be led to believe that, just as sex was invented in 1963,[5] psychology – the systematic study of personality, categorizing the different ways in which people think, act and feel – was an invention of the twentieth century. After all, the Oxford English Dictionary dates the use of 'personality' (meaning 'personal individuality as a subject of psychological and sociological study') to an article in the *Psychological Bulletin* in 1930. In 1937, two studies of personality were published, *Psychology of Personality* by Ross Stagner (1909–1997), and *Personality: A Psychological Interpret-*

ation by Gordon Willard Allport (1897–1967). These marked the beginning of our modern day understanding of personality, an understanding that our poor, superstitious and ignorant ancestors did not and could not have – or so the story goes.

However, it will be unsurprising to find that, as the myth of the conflict of science and religion unduly flatters the modern world, so too does this myth of our novel, psychological insights. For the *OED* also tells us that that great psychological thinker John Wycliffe used 'personality' to mean 'the quality which makes a being human' in 1425.[6] And if the *word* was around in the beginning of the fifteenth century, the *idea* had been around for a lot longer; almost a thousand years longer, in fact.

We have seen how Bosch included in the composition and execution of his painting an advanced and sophisticated political understanding of the world in which he lived. We have also seen how Bosch thought it entirely appropriate to use his cosmological understanding (in the sense of a theory of the universe as an ordered whole) and his scientific understanding (in the sense of how the processes that made up that ordered whole actually worked) in the depiction of the Christ's four tormentors. Bosch used the best knowledge of the day to produce a *Political Circle* and an *Elemental Circle* of interpretation. Now we will see how he also used the best knowledge of his day to provide a *Psychological Circle* of interpretation, or, in the language of his day, a Circle of Temperaments.

In Bosch's day the best understanding of the working of the human body and the human mind was based upon an ancient medical library known as the *Hippocratic Corpus*. The 60 or so books of the *Corpus* were said to have been written by Hippocrates (fl. c 460 BC – c 377 BC). Most historians of medicine now agree that they were actually written by a variety of different authors and ascribed to Hippocrates, whose medical skills were legendary even in his own lifetime. Even so, Hippocrates (or, if you prefer, 'the group of unknown authors collectively known as Hippocrates') was the founder of medicine, and for almost 2,000 years he was the authority for Greek, Roman, and medieval physicians. One of the works from the collection, a book on *Epidemics*, says this about Hippocratic medicine:

> Declare the past, diagnose the present, foretell the future; practise these acts. As to diseases make a habit of two things — help, or at least to do no harm. The art has three factors — the disease, the patient, the physician. The physician is the servant of the art. The patient must co-operate with the physician in combatting the disease.[7]

Hippocratic medicine was marked by three things: 'close observation of symptoms, an openness to ideas from all sides, and a willingness to explain the causes of disease'.[8] It was an immensely humane form of medicine; that is, it focused upon the individual human person. It was 'constitutional'; that is, it examined the physical processes of the body and, by intervening in dysfunctional processes, it sought to restore the equilibrium of health. Illness was:

> . . . an expression of changes, abnormalities, or weaknesses in the whole person; peculiar to the individual, it was 'dis-ease' rather than disease. Such a person-centred view could underwrite a certain therapeutic optimism: relief was in the hands of the 'whole person'.[9]

However, intervention for the sake of showing off the physician's skill or to satisfy the physician's curiosity was forbidden: the Hippocratic oath, in both pagan and Christian forms, did not allow that. It was a holistic approach to illness, and recognized the frequent ability of the body to repair itself. But it also realistically saw that humanity was susceptible to all kinds of diseases and conditions. The body was never still, nor well for long. What could cause such changeableness?

Two men, building upon the work of the *Hippocratic Corpus*, were especially influential in explaining this propensity of the body to fall ill: Galen of Pergamum (c AD 129 – c AD 216) and the Persian physician philosopher Avicenna (c AD 980 – AD 1037). Galen's influence on medicine in general was so great that his system of 'humoral medicine' is often called 'Galenism'.

Galenism shared in the same philosophical underpinnings as Platonic/Aristotelian elemental science. As above, so below was the epitome of elemental science, and as above, so below, so within each person was its application to the individual. In short, to understand Galenism we need to understand that it is part of a holistic medical-scientific approach to the world and individual.

The practical working out of elemental science and its astrological implications can be seen in the prosaic ephemera of a barber's shop. We all know the origin of the traditional red and white striped pole outside gentlemen's hairdressers today. In the Middle Ages barbers were the only people willing to undertake surgical operations; physicians believed such practical activities to be both beneath them with their years of training, and ineffective in comparison with treatment by medicines (in the days before effective antiseptics or even a systematic understanding of infection, they were probably right). Even so, one of the most common remedies for any sort of illness, from 'feeling a little under the weather' right up to plague, was for the patient to be bled. An incision was made in the appropriate part of the body (based upon the nature of the illness and the time of the astrological cycle), blood drawn off, and the humours in the patient's body thus brought back into balance.

Barbers were the men trained to carry out this treatment, and the striped poles were supposed to remind their customers of blood and bandages.

However, it was not possible merely to stroll along to a barber and ask to be bled. The interconnectedness of all things for medieval science meant that some days were more propitious than others for bleeding: days in the common calendar (that is, according to the day of the year and state of the stars), and days in a person's own individual calendar (that is, according to the individual's own horoscope). Horoscopes were thus a necessary part of the surgeon's training, for a person could only be bled on a day appropriate for their zodiacal star sign, birth planet and temperament. To help with the complexity of the necessary calculations (like doing the divisions by 19 required of the Easter calculations in the Book of Common Prayer), the barbers' union in York produced an almanac for its members, the *Guildbook of the Barber Surgeons of York*, now in the British Library (Egerton MS 2572). Handy tables, and aides memoire allowed the busy surgeon to get on with the lucrative business of bleeding his customers dry. One of these tables is shown on folio 51 of the *Guildbook*.[10] In the centre we can see a *volvelle*, a circular scale from which the days of the month are aligned with the days of the zodiacal year. Around the *volvelle* are four saints, clockwise from top left, St John Baptist (holding the Lamb of God, his symbol), St John the Evangelist (holding a chalice and serpent), St Damian (holding a box of ointment), and finally St Cosmas (holding a flask). These last two were brothers, martyred under the Emperor Diocletian in the early fourth century. They were physicians and practised without charging for their services. Because of this charity, they drew many of their patients to Christianity, and were known as 'the Silverless'. Curiously, that didn't prevent them from becoming the patron saints of doctors, barbers and surgeons!

So we can see in the handbook of the Barber Surgeons of York how the Zodiac affected medical intervention. In humoral medicine every function of the body and mind was ultimately a physical function. Each physical function of the body possessed one of four 'qualities': hot, cold, wet or dry. The balance between these qualities was unique to each individual. What was appropriate for one person would not necessarily be so for another. The purpose of medicine was to find the specific balance for each individual and to maintain it. Galen taught that the qualities of the body were maintained by the interaction of four fluids in the body: the *humours* (from the Greek word *chymos*, which literally meant 'juice' or 'sap' and metaphorically 'flavour'). Each of these fluids was naturally found in the body in varying quantities for each person. If the fluids were imbalanced, then that person would become ill: Galen called this *dyscrasia*. The balance of the humours could be seen in a person in two ways: the outward appearance (or 'complexion') and the personality type (or 'temperament'). The four humours were yellow bile, phlegm, black bile and blood itself.

Yellow bile was said to be produced by the liver, and secreted in the gall bladder. It was also known as 'choler'. Along with phlegm, it was one of the potent, active humours, perhaps because it was usually only seen when the body was ill. According to Galen, mania was caused by an excess of yellow bile, boiling in the brain.

Phlegm was any whitish secretion of the body. Avicenna described five varieties: sweet, salty, acid, watery and mucilaginous.[11] The brain was the organ most closely associated with phlegm, perhaps because the organ and the fluid shared a similar colour and texture. Phlegm was thought to be the cause of epilepsy. *On the Sacred Disease*, one of the Hippocratic texts, explained that, if phlegm blocked the airways, epilepsy was the result, as the body convulsed in an effort to clear the blockage: 'The patient suffers all these things when the phlegm flows cold into the blood which is warm; for the blood is chilled and arrested. If the flow be copious and thick, death is immediate, for it masters the blood by its coldness and congeals it.'[12]

Black bile, again produced by the liver, was found in the spleen. It was sometimes known as 'melancholy', and was thought to be deadly to the human in concentrated form.

Blood occupied a special place in humoral theory. The red liquid in the body was thought to be a combination of pure 'humour blood' and a mixture of the other humours. It was produced by the liquidization of food in the stomach, which in its liquid form, *chyle*, was then moved to the liver. From the liver, the nourishment of chyle was then distributed throughout the body as blood. Sometimes the body would produce more blood than it could healthily use. This excess of blood, known as *plethora*, would stagnate, and its constituent fluids, the humours, would separate and cause illnesses in various parts of the body. The physician could therefore diagnose illness by drawing blood from a vein, in a process known as *phlebotomy* or *venesection*, and allow the blood to separate into its constituent parts. The proportions of humours in the sample would indicate a diagnosis. Treatment of the illness was often the drawing of more blood, to remove the excess humours in the body:

Phlebotomy clears the mind, strengthens the memory, cleanses the stomach, dries up the brain, warms the marrow, sharpens the hearing, stops tears, encourages discrimination, develops the senses, promotes digestions, produces a musical voice, dispels torpor, drives away anxiety, feeds the blood, rids it of poisonous matter, and brings long life.[13]

We can see from this long list of benefits that the humours didn't just affect the physical working of the body. The emotional component of the human person was also subject to humoral imbalance. Aretaeus, a contemporary of Galen from Alexandria, described the emotional effects of such an imbalance of humours. Those who suffered from excess black bile:

> . . . are dull or stern: dejected or unreasonably torpid, without any manifest cause . . . they become peevish, despirited [sic], sleepless, and start up from a disturbed sleep. Unreasonable fears also seize them . . . if the illness becomes more urgent, hatred and the avoidance of the haunts of men, vain lamentations are seen; they complain of life and desire to die.[14]

We have a pleasing picture of the well-rounded physician in Chaucer's 'Prologue' to *The Canterbury Tales*. We are told that:

> With us there was a doctor, a physician;
> Nowhere in all the world was one to match him
> Where medicine was concerned, or surgery;
> Being well grounded in astrology
> He'd watch his patient with utmost care
> Until he'd found a favourable hour,
> By means of astrology, to give treatment.
> Skilled to pick out the astrologic moment
> For charms and talismans to aid the patient,
> He knew the cause of every malady,
> If it were 'hot' or 'cold', or 'moist' or 'dry',
> And where it came from, and from which humour.
> He was a really fine practitioner.[15]

The 'really fine practitioner' would have been able to describe the integrated system of thought that Plato, Aristotle,

Hippocrates, Galen, Avicenna and others provided him. Elements, humours, complexions, temperaments, stars and planets were all bound together in a single matrix, where an understanding on any one level could be transferred to another. Chaucer's doctor could have represented this system in a table of equivalence:

Element	Air	Fire	Earth	Water
Qualities				
(1st/2nd)	Wet/Hot	Hot/Dry	Dry/Cold	Cold/Wet
Humour	Blood	Yellow Bile	Black Bile	Phlegm
Organ	Liver	Spleen	Gall bladder	Brain/lungs
Temperament	Sanguine	Choleric	Melancholic	Phlegmatic
Season	Spring	Summer	Autumn	Winter
Ages	Infancy	Youth	Adulthood	Old Age

Our painting is another way of depicting such a table of equivalence. Bosch gives us four portraits of the human temperaments in our four tormentors.

Look at the green man again. We have seen in the first two circles how he represents the secular powers of Europe, and in the Elemental Circle he takes the position of Fire. He is the action man, forcing the crisis of Christ's Passion to its climax, and so in the Temperament Circle he stands as the *Choleric* man, in whom the forces of yellow bile are out of control. The jut of his jaw, and the grimness of his grip upon the crown of thorns shows that his anger is barely under control. He is about to explode. The choleric temperament tends to domination, especially of those who are phlegmatic. 'They are naturally quick witted,' wrote Nicholas Culpeper, in his paraphrase of Galen's Art of Physic (1652), 'bold, no way shame-faced, furious, hasty, quarrelsome, fraudulent.'[16] Notice how the green man dominates the heights of the painting, positioned above everyone else, and leaning in and down upon the composition. He is in charge.

Look at the dark man, the dog-collared soldier in the pay of the papal family. Recall how in the previous Circle he stood for Elemental Air, controlled by its astrological master Jupiter. The Temperamental equivalent is *Sanguinity*, the temperament controlled by blood and the liver. Springtime is the season of the sanguine, and the sprig of fresh green leaves on his hat reminds us of the fecundity of that time of year. The sanguine temperament was thought to be the best of the four, perhaps because blood was thought to be universally a good thing, provider of warmth, and life, and nourishment to the body. The sanguine person was optimistic, even-tempered, cheerful, open to the needs and experiences of others. 'They are merry, cheerful creatures,' wrote Culpeper, 'bountiful, pitiful, merciful, courteous, bold, trusty . . . A little thing will make them weep, but soon as 'tis over, no further grief sticks to their hearts.'[17] But the sanguine person could also be unmotivated, dreamy, lacking in drive and accomplishment. Is Bosch saying here that the sanguine Church is too willing to let the wicked things happen in the world, even to the extent of allowing Christ to suffer his Passion again, all for the sake of popularity and preoccupation?

Below the dark man is the rose-robed man, who stood for the Jews in the Politics Circle, and Earth in the Elemental Circle. Here he stands for the *Melancholic* temperament, the person afflicted by excess of black bile. Robert Burton (1577–1640), scholar, cleric and depressive, wrote the classic description of this condition in *The Anatomy of Melancholy* (1621). This was a monumental and dazzling work, eventually, after six editions, settling at over 500,000 words, with a bewildering array of quotations, allusions, jokes and epigrams. I like to think that the size and style of Burton's *Anatomy* was an elegant, ironic, riposte to well-meaning busybodies who provide the perennial advice for the depressed: be 'busie to avoid Melancholy. There is no greater cause of Melancholy than idlenesse, *no better cure than businesse.*'[18] Look, says Burton, have I been busy enough?

Burton saw that melancholia was part of the human condition: those who were melancholic were:

> . . . dull, sad, sowre, lumpish, ill disposed, solitary, any way moved, or displeased. And from these Melancholy Dispositions, no man living is free, no *Stoicke*, none so wise, none so happy, none so patient, so generous, so godly, so divine, that can vindicate himselfe; so well composed, but more or lesse some time or other, he feeles the smart of it. Melancholy in this sense is the Character of Mortalitie.[19]

Look at the sad, sour, lumpish features of the rose-robed man. His beautiful clothes, his scholar's robes, his (presumed) health and wealth – none of these can remove the curse and smart of melancholy from him. He knows the weight and the burden of earthly mortality, and even grasping at the one who brings life and light and freedom can do nothing to lighten that weight, if the grasping is done for the wrong reasons, unknowing of whom he grasps.

Finally, look at the old man, with his crescent moon headdress, his watery eyes and dripping nose. He stands for political infidels, and he is Elemental Water. His temperament is ruled by *Phlegm*, the product of the brains and lungs and the watery parts of the body. His season is winter, and the unavoidable fact of old age, approaching death. Phlegmatic people were supposed to be stolid, disconnected from others: 'cowardly, forgetful creatures', says Culpeper.[20] John Harington in his verse portrait of the phlegmatic says:

> Content in knowledge to take little share
> To put themselves to any pain most loath.
> So dead their spirits, so dull their senses are . . .[21]

Dead and dull, the old man rests his hand upon Christ, and with it the coldness of the grave. Bosch is telling us that here is Christ, already entering his great battle with Death.

Bosch has arranged his temperament-tormentors in two diagonals, two lines from choleric to melancholic and from sanguine to phlegmatic. The first diagonal is all about aggression against Christ, the green man in the upper part of the diagonal forcing something onto Christ, the man in rose in the lower part of the diagonal pulling something away from him. The second diagonal is all about (corrupted) sympathy. Hands rest upon Christ, but the gestures are suspect, somehow disquieting: the upper part of the diagonal (the dark man) has a hand resting lightly upon Christ's shoulder, and he is addressing himself to Christ's head, the seat of the rational person, perhaps in words of seduction and capitulation; the lower part of the diagonal (the old man) has his hand resting upon Christ's lap, and although his eyes are upon Christ's face, we somehow feel that his attention is upon Christ's body. Aggression bisected by false sympathy, a cross upon the circle.

The four human temperaments, the four ages of man, the four seasons. All four crowd around Christ, and are part of his suffering. Bosch is showing us how it is not just one type of person who is responsible for Christ's Passion, the 'evil' person, the 'wicked' person, the person 'not like us'. Rather, he says, it is *all* people who are culpable: you, them, me.

Fifty years after Bosch's death this understanding of human character began to die away. A new system of thought, one that rejected Galenism, began to grow: chemical medicine. The most influential leader of this new system of thought was the Swiss physician, alchemist, mystic and iconoclast, Phillip von Hohenheim, better known by his pen name, Paracelsus (1493–1541). Paracelsus rejected humoral medicine and its philosophical underpinnings because he regarded it as pagan. He wished to replace it with a Christian philosophy, and thus he is sometimes known as the 'Luther of medicine'. He rejected the teaching of the established medical schools, and instead advocated travel to seek knowledge: 'I have not been ashamed to learn from tramps, barbers and butchers,' he proudly boasted.[22] He made his name as the town physician of Basle in 1527 by publicizing a series of lectures to rival that of the medical school: he stood in the university square and publicly burnt the books of Galen and Avicenna. His medical theory rejected the idea of *internal* imbalance: instead he argued that illness was caused by *external* factors. For Paracelsus these external factors were derived from the universal nature of matter: human beings were made from the same stuff as the heavens and the earth: minerals, astral seeds (*seminia*) and astral elements (*essentia*). There were three fundamental substances: salt, sulphur and mercury. This led him to develop chemical remedies for specific diseases. For example, gout, which in Galenism was thought to be a flow of the humours to the foot, Paracelsus argued was rather caused by an excremental salt (tartar) coagulating in the joints. Such salts were caused by impurities in the water supply, which was why Switzerland, with its exceptional purity of water, saw no instances of gout.

Paracelsus's influence grew after his death, and by the time Petrus Severinus published his *Medical and Philosophical Ideas* in Basle in 1571, the influence of the humoral theory was waning in the face of chemical medicine. It finally died in 1858 when Rudolf Virchow described the mechanisms of cellular pathology. There was no longer any need for the hypothesis of the humours. The integrity and interconnectedness of physical medicine and psychological medicine which Galenism represented was broken.

Curiously, just as the physiological explanation of humours died out, a psychological interest in type and temperament began to develop. Sigmund Freud (1856–1939) was the most important figure in the new mapping of human temperaments. For him, with his roots in neurology and clinical treatment of those suffering from mental illnesses, the human personality was divided into a three-way battle between the id (the most primitive agency, driving the body away from pain and towards pleasure, using especially the instruments of sex and aggression), the ego (the agency most readily accessible to the individual and that which is identified as the self, 'I'), and the superego (the ethical agency of human personality that develops in response to external stimuli, taught how to behave by social factors, and especially the individual's parents). The emergence of these three agencies was intimately related to the human sexual drive, and the cause of psychological illness was usually to be found in repressed memories of sexual trauma.

Freud's early disciple Carl Gustav Jung (1875–1961) broke with his teacher over this theory of neurosis. For Jung a more important factor was the *typology* of the human psyche. He distinguished two types of personality: extraverted (outward-looking) and introverted (inward-looking). Jung published his theory in *Psychological Types* in 1921, a mind-swimmingly learned book: it ranged from the theological disputes of the early Church through Schiller's ideas on aesthetics to depiction of 'types' in biography.

For Jung the two types of human personality were further differentiated by four functions: thinking (the means by which ideas are brought into 'conceptual connection with one another' as an act of the will),[23] feeling (the application of *value* to any external stimulation; 'I like or dislike this'), sensation (the 'perception of a physical stimulus'),[24] and intuition (the function that 'mediates perceptions in an *unconscious way*').[25] The former two Jung described as rational, because they are 'decisively influenced by reflection' and 'function most perfectly when they are in the fullest possible accord with the laws of reason'.[26] The latter two are irrational, not because they are *without* reason, but because they are *beyond* reason; they are concerned with the accidental, things beyond a certain proscribed system of thought, such as empirical science. Intuition and sensation are 'functions that find fulfilment in the *absolute perception* of the flux of events'.[27] A familiar experience of this function might be in the sudden realization of the missing word in the crossword puzzle, a 'light-bulb' moment.

Jung's interest in type and temperament was shared by other pioneers of psychology – Adickes, Kretschmer, Adler and Spranger. And, alongside 'scientific' psychology, there were more speculative and mystical approaches.

Rudolf Steiner (1861–1925) is mostly remembered today in England as the founder of the Steiner/Waldorf method of education. In his day, though, he was better known as a scientist, architect, social reformer and occultist, the founder of the Anthroposophical Society, which propagated his religion-cum-philosophy that the spiritual world was only accessible to those who had undergone a reawakening of humanity's primal spiritual consciousness.

In a lecture given in Berlin in March 1909, and later published with the English title *The Four Temperaments*, Steiner asserted a theory of temperaments which was axiomatic, a given: 'Temperament, that fundamental colouring of the human personality, plays a role in all manifestations of individuality that are of concern to practical life.'[28]

For Steiner, temperament was the medium by which the two strands of what makes a human being human are fused together in an individual. These two strands are the product of genetic heredity, 'the things that connect a human being to an ancestral line', and the inheritance of the individual's reincarnation, 'those [things] the human being brings with him out of earlier incarnations'. In this way, '[t]emperament strikes a balance between the eternal and the ephemeral'. The working out of this balancing medium was to be found in the effects upon the four parts of the human individual: Steiner believed that every human was made up of four bodies or 'members' – first, the physical body, formed by chemicals and matter, whose physical nature most closely resembled the 'mineral world'; second, the 'etheric body', that which makes the physical structure 'alive', whose separation from the physical body marks what we call death, and parallelled with the life of plants; third, the 'astral body', the seat of human emotions and senses, shared in common with the animal world; fourth, and highest, 'the bearer of the human ego', our unique capacity for self-awareness.

In this Steiner was doing no more than returning to a medieval schema for physical reality. For the medieval philosopher there were four levels of 'consciousness' (although that would not be a word the medieval natural philosopher would himself have used): 'mere existence (as in stones), existence with growth (as in vegetables), existence and growth with sensation (as in beasts), and all these with reason (as in men).'[29]

Steiner's four constituent parts expressed and influenced the temperaments:

In every case, one of the four members achieves predominance over the others, and gives them its own peculiar stamp. Where the bearer of the ego predominates, a choleric temperament results. Where the astral body predominates, we find a sanguine temperament. Where the etheric or life-body predominates, we speak of a phlegmatic temperament. And where the physical body predominates, we have to deal with a melancholic temperament.

We are no longer dealing here with fluids or humours, but a much deeper, spiritual, theory of temperament. Steiner's understanding of temperament remains a lynchpin of his educational method, and Steiner/Waldorf schools use temperament as a way of matching teaching methods to the individual child. However, perhaps because Steiner's other ideas (reincarnation, spiritual realms) were so out of kilter with the prevailing mood of empirical realism, his ideas on temperament found no encouragement within scientific psychology. By 1930, psychology was no longer interested in types: dynamic and behaviourist psychology ruled, in which human actions were best understood as the expression of unconscious desires, repressed experiences, or both.

Temperament was revived by an unlikely mother-and-daughter team, neither of whom had any formal psychological training. Katharine Cook Briggs (1875–1968) and her daughter, Isabel Briggs Myers (1897–1980), shared a lively interest in the work of Jung: Katharine had first read *Psychological Types* in 1923, and corresponded with Jung for ten years before meeting him in 1937. During the Second World War, wanting to contribute to the war effort of the United States and frustrated by the mismatch between individual volunteers and the tasks needed to be done, Isabel remembered her mother's interest in Jung and decided to produce a systematic codification of his types that could be applied to a wide range of people. She developed a 'type indicator', and worked on it until her death. In honour of her mother's contribution she called the scheme the Myers-Briggs Type Indicator. Initially, she faced a great deal of resistance from the professional and academic psychological classes, and it wasn't until 1953 that she was able to begin to give her test to large groups of people, a prerequisite for proving the statistical soundness of her insights. A (critical) assessment of Isabel and her qualifications for this work was given in a memo to the Head of the Educational Testing Service:

> Mrs Myers has dedicated her life and that of her family to the concept of type; she believes it to be a profound and extremely important social discovery. She believes her Indicator provides the way to make this concept useful in educational and vocational guidance, marital and vocational adjustment, elaboration and diagnoses, and therapy of personality problems, etc.[30]

The central idea of the MBTI (as it is called) is that differences between people are caused by differences in the way they *prefer* to interact with the external world (of people, things, experiences) and the internal world (of reflection and ideas). People might be *able* to behave in a variety of methods and manners, but, if allowed a choice, most people will *choose* a particular course of action, a particular way of relating to the external and internal worlds. The choice that people make is an indicator of the personality type in which they are most comfortable. There are four scales in the MBTI, along which the individual's preferences can be plotted, where their 'comfort zone' is found: Where do you prefer to focus your attention? (*Extraversion* or *Introversion*); How do you prefer to take in information? (*Sensing* or *Intuition*); How do you prefer to make decisions? (*Thinking* or *Feeling*); and How do you set yourself towards the outside world? (*Judging*, that is organizing what you experience, or *Perceiving*, that is, enjoying the sensations of experience for their own sake).[31] By answering a series of questions it is possible to weight your preferences for these different modes of interacting with the world. The four scales produce a potential score within one of 16 different 'types', named for the predominating end of each of the four scales. So, for example, if you prefer to focus on the outer world, interpreting the basic information you receive, making decisions by logic and a set of rules, preferring to get things decided and completed, then your personality type would be ENTJ (for Extraversion, iNtuition, Thinking and Judging).[32] As all the Myers-Briggs material makes clear, there are no value judgements in any of these types. No one is better than any other: 'Each type and each individual has special gifts. There is no right or wrong type, no better or worse combination of types in work or relationships.'[33] Even so, there is a highly charged functionalist strand to all modern personality psychology. David Keirsey (who prefers to use 'temperament' rather than 'type' in his classifications, but whose work is otherwise similar enough to Myers-Briggs for them to be often confused) says this:

> Temperament can denote a moderation or a unification of otherwise disparate forces, a tempering or concession of opposing influences, an overall colouration or tuning, a kind of thematization of the whole, a uniformity of the diverse. One's temperament is that which places a signature or thumbprint on each of one's actions, making it recognizably one's own.[34]

Here, temperament is what makes you, you, the mark of your uniqueness in the breadth of humanity. Mary McCaulley, a close collaborator of Isabel Myers, said: 'Each person is unique. An ENFP is like every other ENFP, like some other ENFPs, and like no other ENFP'[35]— rather like the scene in Monty Python's *The Life of Brian* in which Brian addresses the crowd, telling them, 'You're all different!' 'Yes! We're all different!' they chorus back, with one lone dissenter saying 'I'm not.'

There are reservations more substantial than similarities to Python films about this approach to understanding human personality. David J. Pittenger has commented that setting aside the statistical weaknesses in MBTI:

The popularity of the MBTI as a consulting tool most likely reflects the success of the publisher's marketing campaign and the intuitive and simple sounding nature of the instrument's scoring scheme . . . it is probably comforting to learn that one tends to be intuitive and feeling, rather than learning that one has scored high on the neuroticism and low on the consciousness scales.[36]

Which brings us back to Bosch. Think of Myers-Briggs and Keirsey and other representatives of the personality development industry. Look at the self-help shelves in your local Waterstone's. Look at the personal development books bought by the Bridget and Barry Joneses of our day: *Who Moved My Cheese?*, *The Cosmic Ordering Service*, *Men are from Mars, Women are from Venus*, *Women Who Run with the Wolves: Contacting the Power of the Wild Woman*. These books are about us understanding who we are, really, and then celebrating that: 'I'm okay, You're okay'.

This is not Bosch's purpose. For him the green man was perfectly reconciled to his choleric temperament; the dark man was working entirely within his comfort zone as a sanguine person; the rose-robed man had learnt to love his melancholy character; and the old man celebrated the wisdom that came with age and phlegmatism. And yet they were all in the business of crucifying Christ!

Karl Marx said 'philosophers have hitherto only interpreted the world in various ways, the point however, is to change it'.[37] Bosch would concur: 'psychologists have hitherto only interpreted the personality in various ways, the point however, is to change it'. Do not remain trapped in your temperament, Bosch is saying, for if you do, you will end up participating in the crucifixion of Christ. Transform and be transformed.

How that was to be accomplished we will see in our last two circles.

Notes

1 Dawkins, *God Delusion*, p. 53.
2 Leslie J. Francis, 'The Church is in danger of attracting a clergy clone', *The Church Times* (No. 7514), 16 March 2007, pp. 19–21.
3 Ibid., p. 21.
4 Ibid.
5 According to Philip Larkin, in the poem 'Annus Mirabilis' (1967).
6 'Personality', *Oxford English Dictionary*, 2nd edition (Oxford: OUP, 1989). Wycliffe's use is sense A.I.1.a. The psychological sense is A.1.4.c.
7 *Epidemics*, I.11 in *Hippocrates: Loeb Classical Library*, Vol. 1, edited and translated by W. H. S. Jones (London: Heinemann, 1923), p. 164. See also Vivian Nutton, 'The Hippocratic Corpus' in *The Cambridge Illustrated History of Medicine*, edited by Roy Porter (Cambridge: CUP, 1996), p. 58.
8 Nutton, 'Hippocratic Corpus', p. 58.
9 Roy Porter, 'What is disease?' in *History of Medicine*, p. 93.
10 Displayed online at the British Library's 'Collect Britain' website: www.collectbritain.co.uk/dlo.cfm/illuminated/011EGE000002572 U00051V00.htm (accessed 23 October 2007).
11 Nancy G. Siraisi, *Medieval and Early Renaissance Medicine: An introduction to knowledge and practice* (Chicago: University of Chicago Press, 1990), p. 105.
12 *On the Sacred Disease*, 10 in *Hippocrates: Loeb Classical Library*, Vol. 2, edited and translated by W. H. S. Jones (London: Heinemann, 1923), p. 161.
13 A medieval physician, quoted by Sachiko Kusukawa, 'The Medical Renaissance of the sixteenth century' in *The Healing Arts: Health, Disease and Society in Europe, 1500–1800*, edited by Peter Elmer (Manchester: Open University Press, 2004), p. 63.
14 Quoted in Roy Porter, 'Mental Illness' in *History of Medicine*, p. 280.
15 Geoffrey Chaucer, 'General Prologue', *The Canterbury Tales*, verse translation by David Wright (Oxford: OUP, 1985), p. 11.

16 Quoted in Dorian Gieseler Greenbaum, *Temperament: Astrology's forgotten key* (Bournemouth: Wessex Astrologer, 2005), p. 157.

17 Quoted in Greenbaum, *Temperament*, p. 157.

18 Robert Burton, 'Democritus Junior to the Reader', *The Anatomy of Melancholy*, from the Clarendon edition, edited by Thomas Faulkner, Nicholas Kiessling and Rhonda Blair (Oxford: Clarendon Press, 1989), Vol. 1, p. 6. Emphasis in the original.

19 Burton, *The Anatomy of Melancholy*, Subsection 5; Clarendon edition, Vol. 1 p. 136. Emphasis in the original.

20 Quoted in Greenbaum, *Temperament*, p. 158.

21 John Harington, *The Englishman's Doctor*, 1607, a translation into English of *Regimen Sanitatis Salernitanum*, a poetical medical text book from Salerno, Italy, of the High Middle Ages. Salerno was greatly influenced by Arab medicine, and through that, retained access to Greek understandings of human temperament. Quoted in Greenbaum, *Temperament*, p. 159. Harington (1560–1612) was a courtier of Elizabeth I and the inventor of the flush toilet!

22 Quoted in Roy Porter, *The Greatest Benefit to Mankind: A medical history of humanity* (London: HarperCollins, 1997), p. 201.

23 Carl Gustav Jung, *Psychological Types*, Volume 6 of the *Collected Works* of C. G. Jung, revised edition (London: Routledge, 1971) §XI Definitions, ¶830. (References to Jung's *Collected Works* are most conveniently given by paragraph numbers.)

24 Ibid., ¶792.

25 Ibid., ¶770. Emphasis in the original.

26 Ibid., ¶787.

27 Ibid., ¶776. Emphasis in the original.

28 Rudolf Steiner, *The Four Temperaments* (London: Rudolf Steiner Press, 1987). Available online from: http://wn.rsarchive.org/Lectures/FourTemps/19090304p01.html (accessed 6 April 2008).

29 C. S. Lewis, *The Discarded Image: An Introduction to Medieval and Renaissance Literature* (Cambridge: CUP, 1964/1994), p. 93. Lewis directs the reader to Pope Gregory the Great's *Commentary on Job* (*Moralia*), VI.16, and John Gower's *Confessio Amantis* (Tales of the Seven Deadly Sins), Prologus, 945ff: 'Forthi Gregoire in his Moral / Seith that a man in special / The lasse world is properly: / And that he proeveth redely; / For man of Soule resonable / Is to an Angel resemblable, / And lich to beste he hath fielinge, / And lich to Trees he hath growinge; / The Stones ben and so is he . . .'

30 Quoted in Malcolm Goldsmith and Martin Wharton, *Knowing me–*

Knowing you: Exploring personality type and temperament (London: SPCK, 1993), p. 195.

31 See Isabel Briggs Myers, *Introduction to Type: A guide to understanding your results on the Myers-Briggs Type Indicator*, 5th edition (Oxford: Oxford Psychologists Press, 1993), pp. 4–5.

32 See the examples on the website of the Myers-Briggs Foundation. Available online from www.myersbriggs.org.

33 Myers, *Introduction to Type*, p. 30.

34 David Keirsey and Marilyn Bates, *Please Understand Me: Character and temperament types* (Del Mar, CA: Gnosology Books, 1978/1984), p. 27.

35 Myers, *Introduction to Type*, p. 30.

36 David J. Pittenger, 'Cautionary comments regarding the Myers-Briggs type indicator', *Consulting Psychology Journal: Practice and Research*, Vol 57 (3), Summer 2005, p. 219.

37 The 11th Thesis from *Theses on Feuerbach*, 1845.

Circle 4: Devotions

My niece, an attractive and intelligent woman in her twenties, lovingly raised in a family indifferent to organized religion (or even disorganized religion), once told me 'So Jesus died for my sins: that's okay. I'm over it.'

Eleven words which sum up the character of our day and times: indifference. As individuals we are the measure of all that has been and all that is of worth. We are involved with others only in as much as we choose. The claims of the religion, or the historic witness of Christianity may or may not be true, but they have no effect on us. There is no answer to 'So what?' or 'I'm over it'. We can rest where we are. But, if we believe that there is something more to human existence than the sheer brute fact that we are here, we need to find some other rule to live by than indifference. Where can we start to find such a rule?

The first step is to forget the idea that indifference is something new. Martin Luther, who was busy nailing his theses to the church door the year after Hieronymus's death, told this story:

A certain village mayor, when he was about to die, told his pastor, who had been debating the Resurrection with the mayor a long time in an effort to convince him of its reality; 'To be sure, I am ready to believe this, but you will see that nothing comes of it'.[1]

In other words, the greatest challenge the preaching of Christ crucified faced in Luther's day was 'So what?' As for Luther, so for us.

The second thing we have to forget is the idea that Luther was the first and last person to deal with this question; in other words, to think that the corrupted medieval Church had allowed popular piety to decay so far. In truth, 'So what?' has been a perennial question for humanity. Bosch gives us an answer to the question, but to understand his answer we need to learn about the life and work of the greatest Christian spiritual leader of whom you've never heard: Geert Groote.

Geert Groote (or Gerrit Grote or Gerhard Groet or Gerardus Magnus as he was variously known) lived in the Lowlands, on the borders between modern-day Germany and the Netherlands, a hundred years before Bosch. In the middle of the fourteenth century, the valley of the IJssel, a distributary of the Rhine that flowed north towards the Zuider Zee, was as good a place as any to live. Deventer was a trading town on the IJssel, making money since its foundation by the English missionary Lebuinus, Apostle to the Frisians. It was a member of the Hanseatic League, the commercial alliance that brought immense prosperity to the ports of the North Sea from the thirteenth to the seventeenth centuries. Its wealth was based on textiles, dried cod and honey-cakes (*honingkoek*) and, with wealth, went learning. Like 's-Hertogenbosch 60 miles to the south-west, it had a famous Latin School. By 1500 it was the centre of printing for the Dutch Lowlands. Life along the IJssel valley was as settled as life could be.

But Geert was born in the middle of that 'calamitous fourteenth century' as Barbara Tuchman describes it.[2] Europe was convulsed by the Hundred Years' War, the papal schism, the rise of mercenary armies, and popular revolts (the Jacquerie in France in 1358, and Peasants' Revolts in Flanders in 1323–8 and England in 1381). At the same time, in the early part of the century began a climate change so severe that climatologists call it the 'Little Ice Age': glaciers grew, winters lengthened and summers became unreliable. Famines, beginning with a Great Famine in 1315–22, became frequent. In 1346 the Black Death arrived.

Groote was six years old. He had been born to Werner and Heilwich Groote in 1340: his father was a *schepen* (or alderman of the town) and a clothier. Both parents died in 1350, and Geert was brought up by his uncle, Johannes. He was educated in the Latin School, later attended by the young Desiderius Erasmus, and then in Aachen and Cologne. We know that in 1355 he matriculated in the University of Paris, and was awarded a Master of Arts in 1358. Although he was not ordained, he received the income from two church livings to add to the handsome inheritance from his dead parents. This enabled him to continue his studies in the faculty of law in Paris. He was thus the ideal person for Deventer council to employ as an envoy to the papal court in Avignon in 1366; Groote generously refused their fee, but spent most of his time in Avignon petitioning for another living to be awarded him. As his biographer says, 'he walked in the broad ways of the world'.[3]

His life changed when he was living in Cologne in great luxury. Groote was stopped one day by a mystic, who asked him 'Why do you stand here, intent upon empty things? You ought to become another man.' At the time, Groote thought this was nothing but childishness, but when, shortly afterwards, he fell seriously ill, he remembered the mystic's words, and ordered all his books on magic to be burnt. He now knew what he must turn away from, but not yet to what he should turn. That came with a conversation with Henry of Calcer, a friend from his university days in Paris. Henry was now Prior of the Charterhouse in Monnikhuizen, near Arnhem. He appealed to Groote to acknowledge Christ's calling and to renounce the ways of the world, which can only end in death. Groote's heart was 'softened' and he resolved to give up his former ways.[4] He resigned his livings, gave his house as a refuge for poor women, and began to live simply and plainly. He wrote himself a manifesto for his new life: *Resolutions and Intentions, But Not Vows* he called it, and said its purpose was to aid him 'to order my life to the glory, honour, and service of God and to the salvation of my soul':[5]

> In temporal affairs, money, revenue, and books, conduct yourself as a steward, and see to it that you find yourself faithful and prudent. Allot yourself therefore a frugal portion of clothing and food, more to the poor and deserving, and more still for the salvation of souls.[6]

The change in his character was so unexpected and sharp that friends and neighbours thought him mad. Soon he realized that he needed more help to keep him on the way he had begun. He went to the Carthusians, and remained with them for two years.

> Dressing in a long and coarse garment of hair-cloth, totally abstaining from the use of flesh and other lawful things, and passing a considerable portion of his nights in watching and prayer, he forced his feeble body into complete subservience to the spirit.[7]

Eventually the Carthusians encouraged him to take his vocation back into the outside world. He received ordination as a deacon from the Bishop of Utrecht in 1380, and began to preach a renewed call to a serious and holy way of life. In the cities of the Lowlands, his preaching was electrifying:

His magnetic personality, burning zeal to win souls, and power of conviction carried their message straight to the heart. The people came for miles to hear him, many of them leaving their work unfinished and their meals un-touched. The huge churches in the larger cities did not have enough room to hold the surging crowds.[8]

One day in August 1383 he was invited by the Bishop of Utrecht to preach to a synod of the clergy of the diocese. The Bishop wanted Groote to condemn the sin of concubinage, the practice of many priests in living discreetly with their mistresses. Groote did so, but he added warnings against other sins he found among the clergy: sins of heresy, simony, and avarice. His audience was outraged. It didn't help that Groote was only a deacon, and that the laity who heard his sermons were beginning to form themselves into informal groupings for prayer, teaching and mutual support. Who did he think he was? Groote was attacking the structures of the Church, root and branch: he should be stopped. The Bishop withdrew his licence for preaching. Groote appealed to the papacy, arguing that his teaching was rigorous, but orthodox. In early 1384 the Pope found in Groote's favour, and invited him to continue preaching. But, by the time the messenger arrived back in Deventer, Groote was dead: he had visited a friend struck ill by pestilence, and died himself on the afternoon of 20 August 1384. He was 44.

Unlike Caesar, the good that Groote had achieved was not interred with his bones. Even while he was alive Groote realized the effect his preaching had on large numbers of devout men and women. Some of the men were priests, but most were lay. He gathered around him a group of 12 followers, who met regularly in the house of one of their number, Florens Rade-wijns. He was accused by the Dominicans and Franciscans of thereby founding a new religious order without having received permission from the papacy. At the time the accusation was unfounded. This group, and the others like it in the other towns of the IJssel and Waal valleys, we would now call a 'house group' or a 'base community'. Groote's intention, constantly and firmly expressed, was to reform the structures of the Church that were already in place, not to tear them down.

He made this clear in the arrangements he made for the household who had lived in *Meester-Geertshuis* since 1374. He wrote a rule for the women in which he made it clear that they were not a new monastic order; they lived in his house simply so that they might find somewhere to worship God in peace. They were to wear no special clothes, and no nun was allowed to be a member of the house. They should be members of the local parish church, and, although two matrons were appointed to run the house and act as treasurers, none of the inmates were to be prevented from leaving if that was what they wished. All the inhabitants were expected to work for their living; no one, under any circumstances, was to beg.[9] At first they were known as almshouse dwellers, and there was very little in their living which was communal: 'the only thing which the sisters have in common is the use of the house and its upkeep'.[10] They were, most definitely, not nuns. But Groote had to be careful that they weren't seen to be too independent either; the Church had dealt with lay women's religious movements before, and hadn't liked them. It was important that Groot's little house wasn't thought of as a revival of the *beguines*.[11]

No one knows exactly what the word *beguine* means. It might derive from the Flemish 'to beg'; it might be connected with 'albigensian', the Cathar heretics of south-western France loved by Grail conspiracy theorists; it might be a reference to the ancient St Begga of the seventh century.[12] Whatever the origins of the word, by Groote's day it meant something bad, heretical, outside the permissive boundaries of the Church.

The beguines had begun as a spontaneous lay-led movement of women in the thirteenth century. This was a period of religious revival (the Franciscan and the Dominicans were part of the same revival). The contrast between the increasing prosperity of European society with its material inequalities and the Christian ideals of the Sermon of the Mount and the early Church (especially the communitarian model of living in Acts 2) had become a problem for faithful Christians, a problem that could only have a radical solution: living as the Apostles had.

Beguines were not associated with any of the established women's monastic orders, but lived 'lives of apostolic poverty and chastity doing works of charity among the poor and sick'.[13] They retained their rights to property, and were able to leave their beguinages (as their houses were called) if they wished to marry. Some churchmen thought they were a wholly good thing, and encouraged their vocation. Others, concerned about the increasingly subjective nature of their spirituality (direct, unmediated experience of God was encouraged), lobbied for them to be more closely controlled. Popular piety, if unchecked, could lead to social chaos. The Franciscans might be a good thing, it was argued, but what would happen to society if groups like the Humiliati, the Waldensians, and the Dulcinians[14] were allowed to thrive? We can see this debate brilliantly conveyed in Umberto Eco's *The Name of the Rose* (1980/1983).

William of Baskerville is an English Franciscan who visits a monastery in the Italian Alps in 1327, with his German novice, Adso of Melk, the story's narrator. William is at the monastery to study in its famous library, and to participate in a conference between representatives of the Minorites (the Franciscans) and the Pope in Avignon, at this time John XXII. Before the conference can begin, a series of terrible murders are committed in which monks are killed in a way which seem to follow a pattern from St John's Revelation. There appears to be a connection between the deaths, the conference, and the radical movements in the Church of the time. The subject of the conference – whether or not Jesus and his disciples owned their clothes – is really just a symptom of greater conflicts. The papacy was locked in dispute with the German Emperor, Louis IV of Bavaria, who in turn was fighting his cousin, Frederick I (the Fair) of Austria. In these circumstances, Fra Dolcino's ideas are so dangerous, Adso is told, because:

> He said that to bring to an end this third age of corruption, all the clergy, monks, and friars had to die a very cruel death; he said that all prelates of the church, all clerics, nuns, religious male and female, all those who belong to the preaching orders and the Minorites, the hermits and even Boniface the Pope had to be exterminated . . .[15]

The Franciscans are pawns in this struggle. The irony of the situation is made clear by the subtitle that Eco gives the chapter of the conference: 'In which there occurs a fraternal debate regarding the poverty of Jesus'. It was anything but; too much was at stake:

> [Bishop] Alborea, running short on arguments, indicating in a loud voice and with words I dare not repeat his firm intention to pull off the beard of the Bishop of Kaffa, whose masculinity he called into question, and whom he planned to punish, by the logic of an eye for an eye, shoving that beard into a certain place.[16]

With such high stakes, it was no wonder that the beguines, and other lay religious movements, were condemned and suppressed at the Council of Vienne in 1312 (the same council which, to the delight of Dan Brown fans everywhere, condemned the Knights Templar). However, unlike the Dulcinians or the Apostolici or the Fraticelli, the beguines were not a movement that followed a particular leader; they were a localized and decentralized movement, and it continued so long as groups of women came together to live and pray.

Which is why Groote clearly placed his house of godly women under the authority of Church and town in Deventer. He didn't want anyone to think that they were an unauthorized religious order. It wasn't until 1398–9 that the almshouse dwellers became known as Sisters of the Common Life.[17] Noble women had come to live in the house; at first they were turned away as they were not destitute. Gradually, though, daughter houses were founded to accommodate all: Zwolle, Brandes, Kerstenens, Buuksen and Lamme van Dysese, as well as four other houses in Deventer itself. These were all for women: what of the men?

On the last day of his life, the group of disciples came to his death bed. Groote stirred himself enough to tell them:

> My friends, do not fear, and let not your hearts be troubled. You will not have to give up your present mode of life. In order that you may protect your temporal possessions I advise you to build a monastery, where those among you best fit for the monastic life may find shelter and perform their work in peace, while at the same time it will protect the others who prefer to remain in the world.[18]

When asked which monastic rule they should follow, Groote answered Augustinian, for their rule was less harsh than the Carthusians and the Cistercians. Perhaps he was also influenced by his friendship with the Augustinian Canon John Ruysbroeck, who had shown him kindness when he was seeking his own vocation. Under the leadership of Florens

Radewijns (1350–1400), the disciples founded a community at Windesheim, 15 miles from Deventer. It flourished, attracting new members, founding new houses, and incorporating already existing monastic houses under its authority: 6 houses by 1400, 11 by 1420, 20 by 1460, 39 by 1500[19] (a house in 's-Hertogenbosch was founded by 1424). The Windesheim congregation, the Brethren of the Common Life, was not just another religious house among religious houses, it was the spiritual home and exemplar of a whole new religious movement, the *devotio moderna*, the 'modern devotion', the 'new way'.

We are cynical now of movements and products branded 'new' to distinguish themselves from their predecessors: 'New' Labour, 'new & improved' Coca-Cola. However, the New Devout, whether the religious in the monasteries, or laity in the world, deserved their description:

> At a time when all of Europe was calling out for the reform of the clergy and the Reformation would be carried forward by a wave of violent anticlericalism, the Modern Devout quietly began living up to the ideals many were preaching . . . [They] spent their lives in ordered prayer and work.[20]

The New Devout chose to order their prayers and work in four ways. First, they consciously relived, in the imagination, the cycle of Christ's life, teaching and Passion so that Christ might be held at the centre of their lives and they, through beholding him in that way, might represent him to others. Christ within me, Christ before me, Christ shown forth from me, is the New Devotion ideal. Second, they absorbed the witness of holy scripture into their consciousness through both contemplative and community reading. Every member of the New Devotion was encouraged to make a collection of the passages of scripture they found most affecting. The words of scripture, breathed with God's own inspiration, in turn became their own inspiration.

Third, while not averse to scholarship (they were not Know-Nothings), the New Devout put all learning to a purpose: the encouragement of virtue. Groote himself, in his *Resolutions*, wrote:

> Man is corrupted by the honours, favours, and especially the greed that drives everyone. Through the lucrative arts he becomes so tainted and inflamed that his natural uprightness is forgotten and his appetites infected; he no longer looks to the things of God, or virtue, or of bodily good.[21]

Fourth, and most importantly, the New Devout sought to 'develop interiority'.[22] They understood that a whole person was made up with physical and mental faculties, that there was a structure of the mind as well as a structure of the body. They built on the insights of the Greek philosophers, the Fathers (especially St John Cassian) and the scholastics, to help them train the will of the whole person towards Christ. They wanted to have an inner life expressed through actions of the body, and to this end they encouraged a new form of spiritual discipline: the exercise (Latin: *exercitium*; Middle Dutch: *oefening*).

The Brethren did not invent exercises (the Church Fathers and the founders of monasticism were responsible for that), and they weren't the last to use the form (St Ignatius Loyola a hundred years later based much of his *Spiritual Exercises* upon the New Devotion). Originally a military idea (practice for the battlefield), for the Brethren it became universally applicable. Their exercises 'embraced fasting, prayer, meditation, and all the focused devotional activities of religious persons'; in fact, there was no aspect of their lives, corporate or individual, that could not be applied to exercise. Taking from the Franciscans concentrated meditation on the suffering of Christ, they added 'an emphasis of their own on steady progress in battling the vices and acquiring the virtues':[23]

> . . . undertake at some convenient time a diligent examination of yourself and your entire condition. Begin with your inner man, and what moves the power of your soul, how near or far they are from what they ought to be and from that for which God endowed you.
>
> Examine your reason. Think whether it is not in error on many things, whether it is not idle and preoccupied with vain things . . .
>
> Next, examine your memory. See what meditations come forward most frequently, for you think on that which you most love or fear.
>
> Then examine your appetites. Think what saddens you, what disturbs, what gladdens, what brings hope, what you hate . . .[24]

This is a profoundly humane spirituality, both in the sense of being measured on a human scale (setting out a system of behaving and believing that was achievable by people living in the chaos of the fourteenth century), and also in the sense of being gentle with and sympathetic towards the inevitable failing of fallen human beings. Occasionally historians say that Groote and his disciples were 'mystics'.[25] That's not the best way to think of them: mystics spend their lives on mountain tops, in direct spiritual communion with the Divine, ignoring the mortal flesh in which, for the moment, they have found themselves. The Brethren of the Common Life were too *rooted* in life to be mystics. They were disciples, who sought to learn, and through learning, find their way to heaven.

So, the New Devout were serious people, following a serious

vocation. They showed this by their willingness to learn from exemplars of the faith. The priors of the various houses wrote copiously on the history of the movement, and the teachings of the founders, and especially that of Geert Groote. Eventually the ethos of the movement was summed up in a stupendous book by the novice master of the house at St Agniertenberg, just north of Zwolle. He wrote the book in about 1420 for novices joining the house, but it was swiftly seen to be of much wider use: it was applied to life outside the priory walls. Before the invention of printing it was copied thousands of times (we still have 750 of these handwritten copies). First printed in 1472, it is still in print, and has appeared in more than 3,000 editions. The novice master had been schooled in Deventer, although his family was originally from Kempen in Germany. His name was Thomas, more familiar to us as Thomas à Kempis, and his little manual is *The Imitation of Christ*.[26]

It is hard to overexaggerate the influence of Thomas of Kempen and his book. It is probably, behind the Bible itself, and the *Little Red Book* of Chairman Mao, the most reproduced work in human history: Dr Johnson thought that it had been translated into as many languages as there had been months since it first appeared.[27] Although written in Latin it was swiftly translated into the vernacular: the first Middle Dutch translation was completed by 1428, and a partial English translation was made in 1503 by Margaret, Countess of Richmond and mother of Henry VII. Thomas wrote continuously through his ministry at St Agniertenberg, and when he died in 1471, the chronicler of his priory recorded:

He was in the 92nd year of his age, the 63rd of his religious clothing, and the 58th of his priesthood . . . He had an especial devotion to the Passion of Our Lord, and understood admirably how to comfort those afflicted by interior trials and temptations.[28]

The Imitation was originally written as four separate books. It follows the now familiar 'exercise' pattern, aiding the Brothers and Sisters of the Common Life in their meditation upon and journey towards Christ. It is not a linear book, following an arc of argument. Rather it 'unfolds, gradually displaying the patterns of an intricate mosaic'.[29] In fact, it could be said to be a book made up of a series of circles, centred upon the 'sole road to God . . . the power and teachings of Jesus Christ, true God and true Man'.[30] Circles around Christ; is that familiar?

The four books cover, broadly, four areas. First, Thomas describes the necessity for leading a spiritual life, one in which material cares are subsumed to the human need for God. This is not something that can be achieved by the will, or even by techniques of life, but rather by a humble and earnest waiting on God: 'if we rely only on the outward observances of religion, our devotion will rapidly wane'.[31] This leads to a discussion, central to the New Devouts' anthropology and theology (what they believed about human nature and God's nature), on interiority, the inner life:

> He who walks by an inner light, and is not unduly influenced by outward things, needs no special time or place for his prayers. For the man of the inner life easily recollects himself, since he is never wholly immersed in outward affairs. Therefore his outward occupations and needful tasks do not distract him, and he adjusts himself to things as they come. The man whose inner life is well-ordered and disposed is not troubled by the strange and perverse ways of others; for a man is hindered and distracted by such things only so far as he allows himself to be concerned by them.[32]

The third book is the longest. In it Thomas teaches that it is not enough just to be aware of one's interior life: that is solipsism, and is antithetical to the Christian understanding of God's purposes. The New Devout should examine her interior life, and then be prepared for it to change:

> This, then, is the truth, by which vainglory is put to flight. And if heavenly grace and true charity enter in, there will be no envy or meanness of heart, nor will self-love retain possession. Divine charity overcomes everything, enlarging every power of the soul.[33]

Thomas explores how this shedding of vainglory might be expressed:

> . . . resolve to do the will of others rather than your own. Always choose to possess less rather than more. Always take the lowest place, and regard yourself as less than others. Desire and pray always that God's will may be perfectly fulfilled in you.[34]

This finally, is the goal of human living, the 'inward consolation' of the book's title:

> All human comfort is short-lived and empty; but blessed and true is the comfort received inwardly from the Truth. A devout man always bears Jesus his Comforter in his heart, and says to Him, 'Lord Jesus, remain with me everywhere and at all times.' Let this, then, be my comfort, to be ready and willing to forego all earthly comfort. And if Your comfort be lacking, may Your holy will and just trial of my life be my highest consolation . . .[35]

The final book directs the disciple to a faithful, informed, devotion to Christ in the Holy Sacrament. The Devout should earnestly wish to receive communion frequently, in great love, mindful of the love that hung upon the cross for all: 'nothing can comfort me, nor can I rest content in anything created, but in You alone, O my God, on whom I long to gaze for ever'.[36]

The whole of Christian life is described. The Christian is invited to seek the truth and, through God's calling into light and truth, the Christian is able to exercise virtue. Through those virtues, the Christian is able to realize for himself the union with Christ into which he has already been called, and that union is expressed through and consummated by the Holy Eucharist.

It is a puzzle that the book's title is *The Imitation of Christ*, for the spiritual disciplines it offers are not really based upon imitation at all, if by imitation we mean mimicry. Such an impersonation is too much for fallen people to hope to achieve, and the nature of being fallen means that, once we think we can mimic Christ, a millenarian violence kicks in: the Dulcinians thought they had succeeded in imitating Christ, to perfection. No, for Thomas of Kempen, and all the teachers of the New Devotion, Christ was a goal, not the means to the goal:

> The person of Jesus Christ stood central to this New Devotion . . . Their emphasis fell neither on imitation in a strict sense, as in works of mercy, nor on 'mystic union,' as in the teachings of many late medieval authors, but rather on an individual and affective identification with particular moments in Christ's life, chiefly his passion.[37]

Which brings us to Bosch. What connection is there between the New Devout and our painting? We have seen that there was a house of the Windesheim congregation in 's-Hertogenbosch, and that the Brethren were commonly found throughout the Lowlands in the fifteenth and sixteenth centuries. Thomas of Kempen's book would have circulated in the town, and Bosch may even have been familiar with it. But is this all – that Bosch and the Brethren share a common environment?

I think we can say more. We have no record that Bosch was a member of the Brethren of the Common Life, but we do know that he was a member of another, similar, brotherhood, which was greatly influenced by the values of the Brethren. Bosch joined the Brotherhood of Our Lady in 1488.[38] As well as being a kind of 'friendly society', the Brotherhood of Our Lady was part of the:

> . . . impulse to a middle way between the established formal religious orders and a rote religion of the layman as passive spectator at the church's great masses and ceremonies . . . [its adherents sought] a more private, personal and simpler religion which could encompass both laity and those in holy orders — in the world, but not of it.[39]

Then recall Thomas of Kempen's advice in the chapter entitled 'On the Zealous Amendment of our Life':

> Remember your avowed purpose, and keep ever before you the likeness of Christ crucified. As you meditate on the life of Jesus Christ, you should grieve that you have not tried more earnestly to conform yourself to Him, although you have been a long while in the way of God. A Religious who earnestly and devoutly contemplates the most holy Life and Passion of Our Lord will find it in an abundance of all things profitable and needful to him, nor need he seek any other model than Jesus.[40]

Think of that passage with *Christ Mocked* before you, and see if you agree with Richard Foster and Pamela Tudor-Craig that 'the Imitation of Christ could, indeed, be a sub-title for the painting'.[41]

Our previous Circles of meaning have been in a vertical plane, moving around the painting, from tormentor to tormentor. This Circle is different, for Bosch has turned the Circle through 90 degrees. It no longer lies on the vertical plane; now it follows a horizontal path. For the first time the Circle touches the centre and subject of our painting, the figure of Christ. Christ is at one tangent of the Circle, and as it moves out from the frame of the painting, we find ourselves at the other. The Circle has been drawn to include us, separated in time and space from the artist, and time and space from the subject. This horizontal Circle is a supranatural Circle, for it functions not only in the world of space/time but also in the spiritual world, the heavenly realms, the place of the Son.

All this may be so, but the 'So what?' question remains. Thomas of Kempen and Hieronymus Bosch lived a very long time ago. Their days were filled with trouble and sickness, wars and rumours of wars. How can such an 'ancient' devotion to an image, an idealization of an anthropology (the understanding of humanity) and a theology (an understanding of God) be meaningful for men and women of the twenty-first century?

There are two answers to this, perennial, 'So what?' question. The first answer, like Geert Groote, comes from Deventer. Five hundred and forty years after Meester Groote's death in 1484, a young girl came to live in Deventer with her family. Esther Hillesum, known to her family as Etty, was ten years old. Her family (father Louis, mother Rebecca, brothers Mischa and Jaap) moved to Deventer when her father took up the post of classics master at the local secondary school. In one of those pieces of heavenly serendipity the family lived at 9 Geert Grootestraat. Louis was a scholarly man, for whom the world of ideas and learning was of first importance. Rebecca was 'passionate, chaotic, and in almost everything quite the opposite of her husband'.[42] Mischa was a brilliant musician; Jaap had a talent for biology, discovering several new vitamins when he was still a teenager. Etty was also intelligent, and grew into an 'impassioned, erotically volatile, restless and often tormented' young woman.[43] They were Jews.

This was not a problem in Holland in the 1920s and 1930s; after all, the Netherlands had a 400-year-old tradition of welcome and assimilation for Jews. Etty's mother had seen the other kind of life on offer for European Jewry: she had been born Riva Bronstein in Russia, and had fled to Holland after a pogrom. And it wasn't as if the Hillesums were practising Jews.

In 1932, when she was 18, Etty left Deventer and moved the 60 miles to Amsterdam to continue her studies at university. She first read law, and then, perhaps influenced by her mother's heritage, Slavonic languages. By September 1939 she was living in a large household in south Amsterdam, acting as informal housekeeper and occasional lover of Han Wegerif, a widower. She had love affairs with two other, much older men, Klaas Smelik and Julius Spier. Spier was an interesting character and the most influential person in Etty's life. He had worked as a bank manager in his native Germany until he realized he had a talent for palmistry. He trained in psychoanalysis under Carl Gustav Jung in Zurich. At the outbreak of war he fled to the Netherlands, where he practised as a 'psychochirologist', studying personality by the reading of palms. Etty met him in February 1941, and like many women, fell immediately under his spell. She undertook analysis with him, which seems to have involved a lot of wrestling, in various states of undress. It was under Spier's tutelage that Etty began the process of spiritual maturation, which makes her such a remarkable woman. For 18 months she kept a diary, unflinching in its honesty, wit and wonderment.

As the political situation in the Netherlands deteriorated, her brother Jaap managed to get her a job with the Jewish

Council, the agency set up by the Nazis to manage the Jewish population. However, within two weeks Etty had volunteered to be transferred as a Council social worker to the transit camp for Jews at Westerbork, in the north-east of the country. To begin with she was able to travel back and forth to Amsterdam, but eventually, in June 1943, she was sent to Westerbork for deportation.

We have some kind of record of her last months in Westerbork through letters she sent to friends. She paints a picture of degradation and humiliation in 'this utter hell'[44] where people 'live in those big barracks like so many rats in a sewer'.[45] Friends attempted to get Etty away from the camp; she refused, wanting to stay with the parents whom she had found to be so infuriating in their lives before Westerbork.

Eventually, with no notice, the Hillesums were allotted places in the trains going east. A last, heartbreaking postcard was thrown from the transport; farmers found and posted it. In it Etty reports that her parents (the scholarly Louis, the house-proud Rebecca) were with Mischa 12 trucks along: 'Opening the Bible at random I find this: "The Lord is my high tower." I am sitting on a rucksack in the middle of a full freight car . . . We left the camp singing, Father and Mother firmly and calmly, Mischa too.'[46] After three days the train arrived at Auschwitz. Her parents were killed the same day. Etty died, the Red Cross reported, on 30 November 1943. She was 29.

Etty's diary and letters were eventually published in Holland in 1981. They were translated into English in the mid-1990s, and since then, unknown for so many years, she has begun to seep into the cultural mainstream. I am convinced that she will be read in future years for the insight she gives us to the events of the Holocaust, to the development of a strong female voice in human self-understanding, and for what she has to say about a faithful following of God in the midst of horrors.

It was Spier who set her on this path of discipleship. Early in their relationship he told her: 'You are not really as chaotic as all that, it's just that you refuse to turn your back on the time when you thought being chaotic was better than being disciplined.'[47]

The discipline grew within her as the winter of 1941/42 turned to summer. Despite the increasingly dangerous situation for Jews and resisters to the Nazi rule, despite the privations and arrests and bombings and deaths, a kind of spiritual maturity grew within Etty, much to her surprise:

> Am I really sitting here writing things down so calmly? Would anybody understand me if I told them that I feel so strangely happy, not bursting with it, but just plain happy, because I can sense a new gentleness and a new confidence growing stronger inside me from day to day?[48]

The heightened emotions, which she disliked so much in her mother and to which she herself was subject, disappeared, like the dust from the siroccos that plagued her in Westerbork, and in their place was a stillness. It would be wrong to think that this was the product of Etty's own volition: she didn't *will* herself into serenity. It was a co-operative act with God, and, like Thomas Merton ten years later, she surprised herself by this co-operation. Merton put it this way:

> My Lord God, I have no idea where I am going. I do not see the road ahead of me. I cannot know for certain where it will end. Nor do I really know myself, and the fact that I think that I am following your will does not mean that I am actually doing so. But I believe that the desire to please you does in fact please you. And I hope I have that desire in all that I am doing. I hope that I will

never do anything apart from that desire. And I know that if I do this you will lead me by the right road though I may know nothing about it. Therefore I will trust you always though I may seem to be lost and in the shadow of death. I will not fear, for you are ever with me, and you will never leave me to face my perils alone.[49]

Etty expresses it another way:

God is not accountable to us for the senseless harm we cause one another. We are accountable to Him! I have already died a thousand deaths in a thousand concentration camps. I know about everything and am no longer appalled by the latest reports. In one way or another I know it all. And yet I find life beautiful and meaningful. From minute to minute.[50]

This beauty and meaning needed to be expressed. Etty refused to allow herself to rest within this beatific comprehension. She resolved, on the eve of starting work for the Jewish Council:

I shall try to help You, God, to stop my strength ebbing away, though I cannot vouch for it in advance. But one thing is becoming increasingly clear to me: that You cannot help us, that we must help You to help ourselves. And that is all we can manage these days and also all that really matters: that we safeguard that little piece of You, God, in ourselves. And perhaps in others as well. Alas, there doesn't seem to be much You Yourself can do about our circumstances, about our lives. Neither do I hold You responsible. You cannot help us, but we must help You and defend Your dwelling place inside us to the last.[51]

This is akin to Elie Wiesel's play *The Trial of God* (1979), based upon his experiences in Auschwitz as a teenager. One night he saw three rabbis, exhausted by the forced labour of the day, try God on the charge of abandoning his covenant with his people. The rabbis found God guilty, and then said their evening prayers. Similarly, Etty has recognized that there are times in a person's life, or in the events of humanity, in which the only possible way to continue to follow God in a trusting disciple-ship is to take on some of God's role for yourself: in the case of the rabbis, judgement; in the case of Etty, making space for sanctification. She is in good company, for by offering God a means and a place to work in the world, she re-enacts the same hospitality shown by Abraham to God at the oaks of Mamre (Genesis 18). Etty somehow sees it as her responsibility, in the face of so much suffering in the world, to accept God's calling to fulfil the role of love. I am sure Etty would have seen herself in George Herbert's poem, not as the guest, but as the host:

> Love bade me welcome, yet my soul drew back,
>   Guilty of dust and sin.
> But quick-ey'd Love, observing me grow slack
>   From my first entrance in,
> Drew nearer to me, sweetly questioning
>   If I lack'd anything.[52]

Etty was only able to take on this role through a process which she called after the German word *hineinhorchen* ('"hearkening unto" — itself and unto others and unto what binds us to life').[53] This is prayer as something more than the listing of desires, or the patterning of words. It is 'loving attention', recognizing that it is God who is really the hearkener inside her, that 'her' words and 'her' attention are really only a res-ponse of the created to the Creator. As Rowan Williams puts it:

> . . . the self develops as a place where certain realities can find a home, realities that are in one sense very much the inner business of the self and yet are unsought, not generated by the will or the imagination, but implanted — could we say? — by a life history.[54]

It is possible to go further than that. The realities are implanted not just by a life history, but by an encounter with the 'Other', with God. On Good Friday, 1942 (a dating she herself uses) Etty records:

> Something I have been wanting to write down for days, perhaps for weeks, but which a sort of shyness — or perhaps false shame? — has prevented me from putting into words. A desire to kneel down sometimes pulses through my body, or rather it is as if my body had been meant and made for the act of kneeling. Sometimes, in moments of deep gratitude, kneeling down becomes an overwhelming urge, head deeply bowed, hands before my face. It has become a gesture embedded in my body, needing to be expressed from time to time. And I remember: 'The girl who could not kneel', and the rough coconut matting in the bathroom. When I write these things down, I still feel a little ashamed, as if I were writing about the most intimate of intimate matters. Much more bashful than if I had to write about my love life. But is there indeed anything as intimate as humanity's relationship to God?[55]

This understanding of the nature of belief and trust in God has profound implications for our understanding of who we are and who God is (our anthropology and our theology, to use the technical terms). As Rowan Williams says in *Tokens of Trust*:

It is plain that she saw her belief as a matter of deciding to occupy a certain place in the world, a place where others could somehow connect with God through her – and this not in any self-congratulatory spirit or with any sense of being exceptionally holy or virtuous, but simply because she had agreed to take responsibility for God's believability.[56]

This may be Etty's lasting legacy, and it brings us to the second answer to the 'So what?' question, an answer that began in the work of the philosopher Alisdair MacIntyre.

In 1981, MacIntyre, a Scot teaching in the United States, wrote a most unusual book of moral philosophy. *After Virtue* begins with a haunting thought-experiment of a world in which the natural sciences have been calamitously destroyed by the misuse of technology. Science is outlawed, until, in a further reaction, people begin to reassemble the scraps and fragments that are left of scientific knowledge: 'children learn by heart the surviving portions of the periodic table and recite as incantations some of the theorems of Euclid'.[57] Through the book, MacIntyre ponders what could save Western civilization from a similar, moral, disaster, when our civilization has already been hollowed out from the inside by an Enlightenment philosophy which denies that human beings have a *telos*, an end, an ultimate purpose, and asserts that the individual is the whole and sole measure of what is morally right. He finishes the book with the equally haunting thought that Western society has reached a tipping point into a new dark age:

What matters at this stage is the construction of local forms of community within which civility and the intellectual and moral life can be sustained through the new dark ages which are already upon us . . . We are waiting not for a Godot, but for another – doubtless very different – St Benedict.[58]

Then in 1988 the American magazine *Christianity Today* ('the flagship magazine of evangelicalism and the most reliable bellwether of evangelical sentiments')[59] published an editorial by Rodney Clapp.[60] In 'Remonking the Church', Clapp asked if the anti-clerical and anti-monastic strands of modern day American Christianity might have led it to deny itself things of worth and value. He quoted Richard Mouw, president of Fuller Seminary (a conservative evangelical theological college) who questioned whether the evangelical churches would 'benefit from "remonasticization" – the clear and radical witness of a smaller body within the church, calling the entire church to a clearer and more radical witness'. The article has been reprinted and cited many times subsequently, a sign that it has made some connection.

In 1997, Jonathan R. Wilson, an Anabaptist scholar, brought these two ideas together, MacIntyre's watch for the new Benedict and Clapp's advocacy for a remonking, in his book *Living Faithfully in a Fragmented World*.[61] Picking up on MacIntyre's argument for purpose, Wilson argues that the *telos* of humanity is the 'good life' (or, better, the life led well), which is to be found in 'life spent in seeking the good life for man'. Note this well. Wilson makes the good life something to be sought, not something to be achieved or grasped at. The idea of 'practice' is vital to this understanding of the good life: life must be led in scholarship and discipline. Wilson concludes the book with a thought experiment of his own. Perhaps it is unrealistic for MacIntyre to expect a new Benedict, an individual, who can save Western civilization: perhaps it should be a *community*.

Wilson's call has obviously struck a chord, and a series of books have explored this new call to discipleship, a discipleship concerned with justice, mercy and service in community.

The writers are from all denominations and traditions of the Church; some of the most active and passionate advocates were raised in denominations that are historically hostile to monasticism: Richard Foster's Quakerism, Shane Claiborne's interdenominational Congregationalism, and Rutba House's Anabaptist roots.

We can see the connection between the 'New Devotion' of the fifteenth century and the 'New Monasticism' of the twenty-first very clearly in a book like *The New Friars* by Scott A. Bessenecker (published by IVP, historically a very conservative Protestant publishing house). Bessenecker describes the young people who are dropping away from the dominant culture's obsession with material success, shared by the mainstream American churches, and finding Christian discipleship in the service of the poor. He describes the various places of the world in which this service is happening, and ends with an appendix, with six headings suggesting a way to live more simply. *Relationships* should begin in a cultivated closeness with God; hospitality should be exercised regularly; speech should be plain, honest. In your *activities* commitments should be simple; overwork avoided; fasting from 'media, food, people' should be observed periodically. This is only possible if a particular *pace and atmosphere* are encouraged: slow down, say no, enjoy solitude. As for *possessions and finances*, contentment comes from wanting less, and wanting what is useful, not loaded with status: 'learn to enjoy things without owning them', appreciate resources in common ownership, like parks, museums and the seaside. *Appreciation* has a section all of its own; gratitude, joy, creation, encouragement are all factors in the simple life. The suggestions conclude with advice on the *spiritual life*. The word must be central; scripture should be studied and imbued; prayer and simple worship are givens. Finally 'shun anything that distracts you from seeking first the Kingdom of God'.[62] I think Meester Groote could read that list and assent to them all.

Ten years after his book was published, and with the number of New Monastic groups, books, conferences and manifestos growing all the time, Wilson reflected on the impact his work has had. The important thing to remember, he says, is the proper focus or *telos* or end purpose of this way of life:

> . . . the local forms of community for which MacIntyre calls are no longer primarily for the sustenance of intellectual and moral life. Nor are they communities that withdraw from the world to insure their own survival and the flourishing of their members. Rather, within the life of the church a new monasticism exists to sustain knowledge of the gospel of the kingdom that was proclaimed, embodied and accomplished in Jesus Christ. And the communities of the new monasticism exist for the sake of witness to Jesus Christ who is the life and hope of the world.[63]

So we reach our final circle, the person and the presence around whom all our circles and discussions have revolved: Jesus Christ.

Notes

1 Martin Luther, *Luther's Works*, edited by Jaroslav Pelikan and Helmut T. Lehman (St Louis: Concordia Pub. House, 1955–86), Vol 28. *Selected Pauline Epistles: 1 Corinthians 7, 15; 1 Timothy*, p. 102.

2 Barbara Tuchman, *A Distant Mirror: The Calamitous 14th Century* (Harmondsworth: Penguin, 1979).

3 Thomas of Kempen, *Vita Gerardi Magni*, English translation by J. P. Arthur in *The Founders of the New Devotion: Being the lives of Gerard Groote, Florentius Radeevin and their followers* (London: Kegan Paul, Trench, Trübner, 1905), Ch. II.

4 Kempen, *Vita*, Ch. IV.

5 Master Geert, *Resolutions*, in John van Engen, trans. & ed., *Devotio Moderna: Basic Writings* (Classics of Western Spirituality) (Mahwah, NJ: Paulist Press, 1988), p. 65.

6   Master Geert, *Resolutions*, in van Engen, *Devotio Moderna*, p. 75.

7   Kempen, *Vita*, Ch. VII, English translation by Albert Hyma, *The Brethren of the Common Life* (Grand Rapids, MI: Eerdmans, 1950), p. 19.

8   Hyma, *Brethren*, pp. 20–1.

9   Ibid., pp. 49–51.

10   R. R. Post, *The Modern Devotion: Confrontation with reformation and humanism* (Leiden: Brill, 1968), p. 263.

11   The best modern introduction to the beguines, with an emphasis on what makes them special, their spirituality, is found in Saskia Murk-Jansen, *Brides in the Desert: The Spirituality of the Beguines* (London: Darton, Longman and Todd, 1998).

12   See the discussion in E. W. McDonnell, *The Beguines and Beghards in Medieval Culture: With special emphasis on the Belgian scene* (New York: Octagon Books, 1969/1954), Ch. 11, pp. 430–8.

13   Murk-Jansen, *Brides*, p. 11.

14   The *Humiliati* were a penitential movement, originating in northern Italy in the 1100s. At first they were encouraged by the Church as a 'third order', laymen who followed a monastic rule of life, although they were forbidden to preach. They became powerful through the wealth accrued by their work as wool traders and weavers. However, by the beginning of the thirteenth century they were under suspicion of harbouring Waldensian tendencies, and were finally suppressed by St Charles Borromeo, Archbishop of Milan, in 1571.

The Waldensians were named after their founder, Peter Waldo, a rich merchant of Lyons. In a story with striking similarities to that of Francis, he gave away all his possessions and gathered a group around him; they called themselves the Poor Men of Lyons. They were encouraged by the Third Lateran Council (1179), although forbidden from preaching. They ignored the Council's instruction, and evangelized, using a vernacular bible and denying some Church teaching (particularly in the sacraments and purgatory). They were excommunicated and persecuted. Some Waldensian groups survived in France until the Reformation, and became enthusiastic Protestants. It is in this form that they survive today.

The Dulcinians had been inspired by Francis, and the radical group called the Apostolics, mixed with a dash of apocalyptic millenarianism. They were named after their founder, Fra Dolcino of Novara (c 1250–1307), who taught that as they were perfect, it was impossible for them to sin. Dolcino was captured after the Battle of

Mount Rubello and executed by being burnt at the stake on the orders of the inappropriately named Pope Clement V.

15 Umberto Eco, *The Name of the Rose*, 'The Third Day, After Compline' (London: Vintage, 1998/1993), p. 227.

16 Ibid., 'The Fifth Day, Prime', p. 347.

17 See the discussion in Post, *Modern Devotion*, pp. 259–72.

18 Hyma, *Brethren*, p. 53.

19 John van Engen, 'Introduction', *Devotio Moderna*, p. 20.

20 Van Engen, *Devotio Moderna*, p. 23.

21 Master Geert, *Resolutions*, in van Engen, *Devotio Moderna*, p. 67.

22 Van Engen's phrase, in van Engen, 'Introduction', *Devotio Moderna*, p. 27.

23 Van Engen, 'Introduction', *Devotio Moderna*, p. 50.

24 Gerard Zerbolt of Zutphen (1367–1398), *The Spiritual Ascents*, in van Engen, *Devotio Moderna*, p. 253.

25 See, for example, Hyma, *Brethren*, pp. 149f.

26 The most accessible edition of *Imitation of Christ* is in the Penguin Classics series, translated, with an introduction by Leo Sherley-Price (Harmonsworth: Penguin Books, 1952). The critical edition of his works remains *Opera Omnia* (17 vols, 1902–22: Friburgi Brisigavorum: Herder) edited by M. J. Pohl.

27 *Boswell's Life of Johnson*, 30 March 1778 (Oxford Standard Author's Edition, new edition 1952, p. 897).

28 Quoted in Leo Sherley-Price, 'Introduction', *Imitation*, pp. 22f.

29 William C. Creasy, 'Introduction', *The Imitation of Christ: A timeless classic for contemporary readers* (Notre Dame, IN: Ave Maria Press, 1989/2003), p. 24.

30 Leo Sherley-Price, 'Introduction', *Imitation*, p. 12.

31 Thomas of Kempen, *The Imitation of Christ*, I.11, *On Peace, and Spiritual Progress*, in Sherley-Price, p. 38.

32 Ibid., II.1, *On the Inner Life*, in Sherley-Price, p. 69.

33 Ibid., III.9, *How God alone is our True End*, in Sherley-Price, p. 105.

34 Ibid., III.23, *On Four Things that Bring Peace*, in Sherley-Price, p. 124.

35 Ibid., III.16, *How True Comfort is to be Sought in God Alone*, in Sherley-Price, pp. 114f.

36 Ibid., IV.11, *How the Body of Christ and the Holy Scriptures are most Necessary to the Faithful Soul*, in Sherley-Price, p. 205.

37 Van Engen, 'Introduction', *Devotio Moderna*, p. 25.

38 For more on Bosch's membership of the Brotherhood of Our Lady, see Appendix: Who Was Hieronymus Bosch?

39 Gordon Marsden, 'Bosch's "Christ carrying the cross" (Art in Context)', *History Today*, Vol. 47/4, April 1997, p. 19.

40 Thomas of Kempen, *The Imitation of Christ*, I.25, *On the Zealous Amendment of our Life*, in Sherley-Price, p. 64.

41 Foster and Tudor-Craig, *Secret Life*, p. 71.

42 Jan G. Gaarlandt, 'Introduction' to Etty Hillesum, *An Interrupted Life: The Diaries and Letters of Etty Hillesum, 1941–43*, translated by Arnold Pomerans (London: Persephone Books, 1999), p. xviii.

43 Eva Hoffman, 'Preface' to *Interrupted Life*, p. viii.

44 Etty Hillesum, Letter to Christine van Nooten, 21 June 1943, *Interrupted Life*, p. 334. Van Nooten was Etty's Latin teacher from school in Deventer.

45 Etty Hillesum, Letter to Klaas and Johanna Smelik, 3 July 1943, *Interrupted Life*, p. 353.

46 Letter to Christine van Nooten, 7 September 1943, *Interrupted Life*, p. 426.

47 Etty Hillesum, diary entry for 4 July 1941, *Interrupted Life*, p. 40.

48 Etty Hillesum, diary entry for 6 July 1942, *Interrupted Life*, p. 203.

49 Thomas Merton, *The Love of Solitude II*, from *Thoughts in Solitude* (New York: Farrar, Straus and Giroux, 1999/1956), p. 79.

50 Etty Hillesum, diary entry for 29 June 1942, *Interrupted Life*, p. 184.

51 Etty Hillesum, diary entry for 12 July 1942, *Interrupted Life*, p. 218.

52 George Herbert, 'Love (III)', from *The Temple: Sacred Poems and Private Ejaculations* (1633).

53 Etty Hillesum, diary entry for 17 September 1942, *Interrupted Life*, p. 249.

54 Rowan Williams, 'Religious Lives: The Romanes Lecture', Sheldonian Theatre, Oxford, 18 November 2004. Available online from www.archbishopofcanterbury.org/1043 (accessed 6 April 2008). The whole of this lecture is applicable to the Circle of Devotions, dealing as it does with the nature of a 'religious life' and focusing on Etty's refrain of seeking 'to learn how to kneel'.

55 Etty Hillesum, diary entry for 3 April 1942, *Interrupted Life*, p. 129. 'The Girl who could not kneel' was the title of the autobiographical novel that Etty thought of writing. See also p. 90 where she describes herself as a 'kneeler in training'.

56 Rowan Williams, *Tokens of Trust: An Introduction to Christian Belief* (Norwich: Canterbury Press, 2007), p. 23.

57 Alasdair MacIntyre, *After Virtue: A Study in Moral Theory*, 2nd edition (London: Duckworth, 1985), p. 1.

58 Ibid., p. 263.

59 Randall Balmer, *Thy Kingdom Come: How the religious right distorts the faith and threatens America: An evangelical's lament* (New York: Basic Books, 2006), p. 9.

60 Rodney Clapp, 'Remonking the church', *Christianity Today*, 12 August 1988, Vol. 32/11, pp. 20–1.

61 Jonathan R. Wilson, *Living Faithfully in a Fragmented World: Lessons for the church from MacIntyre's After Virtue* (Harrisburg: Trinity Press International, 1997).

62 'Appendix A: Suggestions for Simple Living', in Scott A. Bessenecker, *The New Friars: The Emerging Movement Serving the World's Poor* (Downer's Grove, IL: IVP, 2006), pp. 181–3. Richard Foster (not the Richard Foster who collaborated with Pamela Tudor-Craig on *The Secret Life of Paintings*) was the first Protestant pastor in the modern era to re-present spiritual exercises to his church community as a worthwhile, even necessary, discipline. His book, *Celebration of Discipline: The Path to Spiritual Growth* (London: Hodder & Stoughton, 1980), was first published in 1978, and has now sold more than one million copies. *Christianity Today* listed it as one of the top ten books of the twentieth century (along with C. S. Lewis's *Mere Christianity*, and Dietrich Bonhoeffer's *The Cost of Discipleship*). Foster is the founder of Renovaré, a para-church organization intended to help individuals follow a 'practical strategy' in a 'balanced growth into Christlikeness': available online from www.renovare.org. Again, the similarities with the aims of the New Devotion are striking.

63 Jonathan R. Wilson, 'Introduction', in The Rutba House (ed.), *School(s) for Conversion: 12 Marks of a New Monasticism* (Eugene, OR: Cascade Books, 2005), p. 2.

Circle 5: Quiddity

Success has many fathers, failure is an orphan, and wisdom is only found far, far from home.

This aphorism has been wittily dissected by England's greatest living satirist, Terry Pratchett. If you only knew him by the covers of his 'Discworld' books, with their lurid pictures and punning titles, you might not believe Pratchett could be such a thing. But he uses the fantasy genre to test (sometimes to destruction) the complacently held ideas and opinions of our time. His critique of organized religion, especially in *Small Gods* (1992), is serious, persistent, and much more effective than anything produced by Richard Dawkins, all the more so for being camouflaged in a rollicking tale with jokes.

The 26th Discworld book, *Thief of Time* (2001), begins high up in the mountains at the hub of the world, where snow lies all year round, and temples and monasteries guard the head of every valley. Just as 'coal country' produces coal, and 'cattle country' beef, this is 'enlightenment country', where the monks seek 'the essence of being and the nature of the soul. They make wisdom.' In the most inaccessible valley of all live the History Monks of Oi Dong monastery, founded by the great mystic Wen. Curiously though, the most revered man in the monastery is the cleaner, Lu Tze. The secret of Lu Tze's power comes from following his own Way: 'It is the Way of Mrs Marietta Cosmopilite, 3 Quirm Street, Ankh-Morpork, Rooms for Rent, Very Reasonable'. Pilgrims travel many thousands of miles from

Ankh-Morpork, the greatest city on the Discworld, to the monastery seeking enlightenment; it seemed only reasonable for Lu Tze to make the reverse journey. He sought not enlightenment but perplexity ('After all, enlightenment begins where perplexity ends'), and he found it in the boarding house of Mrs Cosmopilite, a seamstress and a woman full of 'bottomless wisdom'. Lu Tze learnt perplexity at Mrs Cosmopilite's feet, and brought back to his monastery such gnomic utterances as 'I was not born yesterday', 'It does you good to get out in the fresh air', and 'You never know what's going to turn up.'[1]

By the mind-numbing banality of Mrs Cosmopilite's 'philosophy' Pratchett imagines the commonplaces of our own culture treated as koans of wisdom in another. He satirizes the perpetual human need to find wisdom and enlightenment in any place other than your own. Wisdom only comes after a long journey.

Your attitude to the Way of Mrs Cosmopilite will determine your response to this last Circle of our painting: is it possible to find wisdom close to home, or is wisdom, no matter how banal it might seem, only to be found a long way away?

There is no such thing as a 'Christian' answer to this question, for the Christian tradition has oscillated between the two. Sometimes Christians have believed that the deepest, truest understanding of their faith was to be found in the local and particular; sometimes true wisdom could only be got from the distant and the universal.

This oscillation is the outworking of the Christian understanding of the Incarnation. The doctrine of the Incarnation taught that the cosmos was created through the loving action of God in his Logos, or Word or Wisdom, and this transcendent part of the Godhead was born as Jesus to Mary in a particular place and at a particular time. This idea was central to the medieval understanding of God, the world and humanity. It determined the way in which medieval people looked at the whole world. They were:

> . . . preconditioned by the dogma of the Incarnation, and the philosophy of 'realism' that underlies it, to find the ideal with the material, the beautiful within the ugly, the moral and peaceful in the midst of violence and disorder . . . Since everything was of divine creation, medieval intellectuals had no doubt that all the pieces would ultimately fit together in an idealistic, morally committed structure. Whatever they saw or experienced was part of a divine manifestation.[2]

Once you accept that God could, and has, worked through the material nature of the world to effect the salvation of mankind then the way you look at the world is necessarily altered. If God has chosen to become human, it is not possible to condemn the material world as utterly 'beyond God': rather, the material world becomes a sign and a means of God's work in the world. Christians say that God is somehow present in the material world in a way that is not open to religions which teach an unbridgeable gulf between God and creation.

The line between transcendent and immanent, God 'out there' and God 'in here', becomes fuzzy, and so certain times and places were believed to be especially open to the presence of God. Places become holy, people become holy, times become holy. There is a 'particularity' to the Christian understanding of God.

That is one consequence of the Incarnation. The other focuses on the *scandal* of the particularity. God worked his purposes in creation uniquely in the person of Jesus Christ. To encounter God in the person of Jesus Christ is qualitatively different from any other encounter with God before or since. Because of this radical difference, Christianity has taught that

Jesus Christ was not (just) a good man, nor a man blessed by God nor an inspired teacher. Jesus is God. The Church takes as its model Thomas, who when he encountered the risen Christ, did not respond 'This is the proof of the ethical teaching you taught us!' or 'Now I understand the moral component of your ministry!' but rather, simply and decisively, 'My Lord and my God!' (John 20.28).

Of course, to say that the man Jesus Christ is unique in this way is also to say something about the world. The fact that God was incarnated in the person of Jesus Christ, and that this Jesus was resurrected, ascended and glorified, meant that Jesus 'eclipses all holy places and himself becomes the ultimate holy place. There is no place on earth which mediates God's presence in an assured way: that alone can be found in Christ. Thus to be "in Christ" is already to be in the holiest place.'[3]

So, the Incarnation works in two modes: in one mode, we can say that God works through the material world, and therefore the material world 'is good'. In the other mode, we can say that God works through Jesus Christ in the material world, and it is only in relationship to him that the material world can unreservedly be said to be 'good'. This is an important distinction to remember. Christianity has oscillated between these two positions over the course of its history. The whole truth is not to be found in one or the other, because to hold one position, excluding the possibility of truth in the other, is to refuse something that has in itself the potential to embody truth. Distorting the whole truth by paying exclusive attention to one small part of the truth is called 'heresy'.

But we have to remember that the earliest Christians recognized the importance of paying respect to the particularity of Jesus's life, ministry, and especially, his Passion. After all, Pontius Pilate is the only human, other than Mary, who gets a namecheck in the creeds, and the earliest Christian proclamation of the Good News of Jesus Christ was centred upon

Christ's suffering and death. Peter, in the sermon on the day of Pentecost, tells the crowds:

> . . . this man, handed over to you according to the definite plan and foreknowledge of God, you crucified and killed by the hands of those outside the law. (Acts 2.23)

For the early Christians it was important to explain why *this* man, and *this* suffering, and *this* death were so important. What was different from all the other men and deaths? The significance was explained most powerfully using *story*.

There are rhetorical advantages in proclaiming the Good News through the use of story, compared with explanations of, for example, fulfilment of Jewish Law (the letter to the Hebrews), Greek philosophy (Paul's sermon in Acts 17) or Wisdom literature (John 1). Jesus's suffering tells a story, with an order, and a satisfying sense of drama: betrayal is followed by trial, punishment, execution. In the Gospel accounts we find true *narratives* in which it is possible to see the development of the story, and the motives of a cast of characters; not just Jesus, but Pilate, Judas, Peter, Annas, and the minor characters like Barabbas, Simon of Cyrene and Malchus (whether or not the narratives are *true* is a different question). Each of the four Gospel stories shows a general similarity in the structure of the story, but sometimes there are differences in detail or emphasis which grew from the needs of the Gospels' differing audiences. For example, Matthew and Mark show Jesus abandoned by his human disciples, and facing his sufferings with only his faith in God the Father to strengthen him. The human antagonists are negatively portrayed: 'All of them deserted him and fled' (Mark 14.50 parallel with Matthew 26.56b). Jesus's desolation is shown as absolute: all witnesses against him are false, all the judges are corrupt and he is subject to mockery on the cross, from which his only words are 'My God, my God, why have you forsaken me?' (Matthew 27.46 ‖ Mark 15.34) But in the end, God acts to reverse the isolation of the Son: the Temple veil is torn, a Roman recognizes Jesus's true nature.

In Luke's account, Jesus's followers are portrayed more sympathetically. Jesus tells them they have been faithful to him throughout his ministry (Luke 22.28); when they fall asleep in Gethsemane it is through grief, not want of courage. Even Jesus's enemies are not so wicked: the trial before the Sanhedrin has no mention of false witnesses, and Pilate proclaims Jesus to be innocent three times. On the way to Golgotha Jesus is met by the weeping women of Jerusalem and he is accompanied by a penitent thief. On the cross he is able to pray for forgiveness for those who torture him, and his death is a tranquil surrendering of his soul into God's safe keeping.

For John, Jesus is a king in control. In his prayer in the garden he does not pray for the moment to pass him; the Passion is the purpose of his life and being. At his arrest the Temple guards fall to the ground when Jesus describes himself with the divine 'I AM' (John 18.6). He refuses to engage with the questions of the High Priest, saying that his teaching in the Temple was open enough and clear enough for his enemies to know who he is. He even refuses to acknowledge the power Pilate holds over him: 'You would have no power over me unless it had been given you from above' (John 19.11). He carries the cross to Golgotha himself, and completes the prophecies about the Messiah in his own time, and under his own control: 'After this, when Jesus knew that all was now finished, he said (in order to fulfil the scripture), "I am thirsty."' (John 19.28). His burial is prepared, like that of a king's, with a wealth of spices.

Recognizing these differences in emphasis and detail, it is not surprising to note similar differences in the way the Gospels report the abuse, verbal and physical, to which Jesus was subjected. (We touched on some of these differences in Circle 1 above.) All told, the Gospels record four separate episodes of abuse: first, by the Temple guards and crowds associated with the Jewish trial; second, by those of Herod's court when Jesus is transferred to his jurisdiction; third, by the Roman soldiers as part of the trial before Pilate; fourth, by the soldiers, thieves and crowds during the crucifixion itself. Raymond Brown has pointed out that the first and third episodes differ in the 'proportionate space given to mockery and abuse';[4] in other words, in the Jewish trial abuse is more prominent than mockery, whereas in the Roman trial it is the other way around. In the Jewish trial, Jesus is mocked as a false prophet: 'Then they spat in his face and struck him; and some slapped him, saying, "Prophesy to us, you Messiah! Who is it who struck you?"' (Matthew 26.67–68).

In the Roman trial, he is mocked for the claim (whether by him or by his supporters is the moot point in John's account) of his political pretensions, mocked as a false 'king of the Jews'.

All four Gospels use a variety of words to describe this abuse. Raymond Brown tabulates them in the original Greek: Jesus is mocked (*empaizein*), sneered at (*ekmyktērizen*), reviled (*oneidizein*), arrogantly mistreated (*hybrizein*), treated with disdain (*exouthenein*), flogged (*phragelloun*), scourged (*mastizein*), chastised (*paideuein*), beaten (*derein*), hit (*paiein*), struck (*typtein, kolaphizein*), stabbed (*nyssein*), slapped (*rapizein*) and spat at (*emptyein*).[5]

Which abuse is most fully depicted in our painting? At first it seems clear, as the subtitle of the painting tells us: *The Crowning with Thorns*. There is only one episode in which Jesus is crowned with thorns, in which he is mocked and abused for being a pretend king, and that is the abuse of the Roman trial.

This episode is reported in Matthew, Mark and John. Luke is silent on the matter of how the Romans abused Jesus.

Instead, he inserts into the Roman trial a curious episode in which Jesus, discovered by Pilate to be a Galilean, is sent to the court of the Roman's client king of Galilee, Herod Antipas. Conveniently, Herod's court is in Jerusalem, presumably for the festivities of Passover. Before Herod, Jesus is questioned, abused, mocked and sent back to Pilate:

> When Herod saw Jesus, he was very glad, for he had been wanting to see him for a long time, because he had heard about him and was hoping to see him perform some sign. He questioned him at some length, but Jesus gave him no answer. The chief priests and the scribes stood by, vehemently accusing him. Even Herod with his soldiers treated him with contempt and mocked him; then he put an elegant robe on him, and sent him back to Pilate. (Luke 23.8–11)

There is no crown at Herod's palace, only an 'elegant robe'. The Greek word is *lampros*, and it means shining or white, a symbol then, as now, of purity and triumph and virtue. For Luke this is an unwitting confirmation by Herod of Jesus's true identity.

But what are the other Gospels' accounts of the Roman abuse? This is Matthew's version:

> So when Pilate saw that he could do nothing, but rather that a riot was beginning, he took some water and washed his hands before the crowd, saying, 'I am innocent of this man's blood; see to it yourselves.' Then the people as a whole answered, 'His blood be on us and on our children!' So he released Barabbas for them; and after flogging Jesus, he handed him over to be crucified. Then the soldiers of the governor took Jesus into the governor's headquarters, and they gathered the whole cohort around him. They stripped him and put a scarlet robe on him,

and after twisting some thorns into a crown, they put it on his head. They put a reed in his right hand and knelt before him and mocked him, saying, 'Hail, King of the Jews!' They spat on him, and took the reed and struck him on the head. After mocking him, they stripped him of the robe and put his own clothes on him. Then they led him away to crucify him. (Matthew 27.24–31)

Mark and Matthew are substantially in agreement. For them the mockery takes place at the end of the trial and as the first step in the punishment. This seems to accord with what we know of Roman practice. The Jewish Roman historian Josephus tells us that following a riot in Jerusalem (c AD 65) the Roman procurator Gessius Florus ordered 'peaceful citizens' to be scourged then crucified: 'No one had ever before dared to do what Florus did then — to scourge men of equestrian rank before the judgement-seat and nail them to the cross, men who were indeed Jews, but all the same enjoyed Roman status.'[6]

However, in John's account the flogging takes place in the middle of the trial. The Jewish crowds have refused to accept Pilate's offer of the Paschal release: they want Barabbas to be freed. So Pilate has Jesus flogged and mocked. It is only then that the governor begins to lose control of the situation. He presents the ridiculed and beaten Jesus to the crowds ('Here is the man!', John 19.5), and the crowds are unimpressed. They demand that Jesus be crucified still. And Jesus is unimpressed. He refuses to answer where he is from. He tells Pilate that the power exercised by the Roman is only that power that has been allowed to him from above (in John's Gospel 'above' is the symbol for heaven and the power of God).

Pilate, either frightened by Jesus's control or impressed by his innocence, attempts to release him. But the crowds will have none of it. They claim an allegiance to the emperor greater than that of Pilate: anyone who fails to do the emperor's law is guilty of rebellion against the emperor. Pilate must fulfil what the emperor requires. Here Pilate must surely have remembered that, under Roman law, to claim to be a king was a capital offence, originally outlawed by Julius Caesar in 46 BC and reinforced by Augustus in 8 BC. The crime was called *laesae maiestatis* (lese-majesty), causing injury to the majesty of the emperor.[7] It grew to be a wonderfully useful 'catch-all' offence, covering treason, insurrection, rebellion on one extreme to offences against public morality and decency on the other. Tacitus even tells us that adultery became *crimen laesae maiestatis* (*Annals* 3.24). In this way, the Lex Julia functioned like the catch-all charges of offences against the dignity of the state imposed in the totalitarian states in our day. For example, in March 2007, Oliver Jufer was jailed for ten years by a Thai court for insulting the king. His crime? When refused another drink on the public holiday to celebrate the king's birthday he had daubed graffiti on a portrait of the king. The judge treated him leniently: the normal tariff would have been 75 years.[8]

Jesus was guilty of *laesae maiestatis* because only the emperor had the power to appoint kings of the Jews. This is what Augustus had done with Herod the Great in 30 BC and what Claudius would do for Agrippa in AD 41. But the Lex Julia was a double-edged sword for those charged with enforcing it. It was perfectly possible for a magistrate or governor to be found guilty under lese-majesty for failing to enforce the law:

> . . . the emperor's mandate to administer justice was regarded as binding them, too, to do so in every case that came before them, and to decline or neglect to try criminals . . . would signify contempt of the emperor's command.[9]

No wonder it is the last straw for Pilate when the crowds cry, 'If you release this man, you are no friend of the emperor.

Everyone who claims to be a king sets himself against the emperor' (John 19.12). He hands Jesus over to be crucified.

Whenever the abuse took place, Matthew, Mark and John agreed that Jesus was scourged, or flogged. There is little point in trying to work out exactly how he was flogged. Roman descriptions of the various techniques and gradations of flogging (rods for freemen, sticks on soldiers, leather thongs on others) were for Roman citizens in Italy. This was a province in tumultuous times. Neither should we look to the Jewish law for how Jesus was treated. The famous account by Paul of how he received the legal punishment of scourging, 40 lashes less one (2 Corinthians 11.24), has led many people, not least Tim Rice and Andrew Lloyd-Webber (in *Jesus Christ Superstar*), into thinking that Jesus was whipped 39 times. But Paul's punishment was under Jewish law, imposed by Jewish judges. The Gospel writers all agree that Jesus was whipped by Romans; why would they take any notice of Jewish techniques of punishment when they had enough ingenuity and cruelty of their own? So, the honest thing to say is that we don't know how Jesus was scourged, or how many times. We can assume that it was not a token punishment. The Romans didn't do token.

Following the whipping, Jesus was mocked. Why? He had been severely beaten and he was about to be crucified. Why did he need to be ridiculed as well? What could be a worse punishment than crucifixion and, when the punishment was crucifixion, why was there any need to add more humiliation?

A clue comes in the trouble the Romans took to identify Jesus to the crowds who gathered to watch him on the crucifixion hill. Above his head was nailed a sign identifying him as 'The King of Jews' (in three languages, John tells us). The Romans didn't just want to kill a man, they wanted to kill an idea as well. Jesus of Nazareth was condemned to death, and so too was any man who took upon himself the authority that properly belonged to the emperor. This idea didn't fade with the end of the Roman Empire: in our own country, gallows were set up at crossroads and market places so that passers-by might know what happened to men who offended against the king's peace and king's law. Troublemakers were eliminated and with them, it was hoped, would go the trouble they had brought.

What of the crown? How does that relate to the mocking Jesus received from the soldiers? Matthew and John use the same Greek word, *akantha*, thorn plant, to describe the material from which Jesus's crown was made. What was the crown of thorns?

We should remember that in the first century AD the royal insignia was not the high-browed crowns of later medieval kings. Royalty were marked out by diadems or wreaths. Sometimes monarchs were depicted with diadems that were decorated with the rays of the sun, radiating out from every side: Brown tells us that Augustus, Tiberius and Caligula, all emperors of this period, were so portrayed. The Greek word for radiate was *aktinōtos*. Perhaps Mark's word for the crown, *akanthinos*, was a play on this, telling his Christian readers that the soldiers said more than they intended about the nature of the condemned man. As for the plant itself, there is no general agreement. The great botanist Linnaeus (Carl von Linné, 1707–1778) thought that *Ziziphus spina Christi L.* was the right shape, and so gave it a name which reflected that belief. Unfortunately it was unlikely to be growing on the heights of Jerusalem. *Poterium spinosum L.*, the 'thorns' of Isaiah 34.13, could possibly be formed into a helmet-like tangle (as worn by Robert Powell in *Jesus of Nazareth*). A member of the acanthus family, *acanthus spinosus*, bear's breeches, could conceivably be woven into a wreath (the effect that Mel Gibson went for in *The Passion of the Christ*). In the end, the question of exactly which plant was hastily picked by Roman soldiers is not important. It seems, from both Roman and Gospel sources, that the important thing here was the crown, not the thorns. The thorns were not an attempt to inflict more bloodshed upon Jesus, despite what some late medieval depictions and Mel Gibson portray. The crown was an attempt to humiliate Jesus, to ridicule his pretensions to political power, and to condemn his ideas.

The title nailed to the cross, which John explicitly tells us was the work of Pilate ('What I have written I have written.' John 19.22), was the official humiliation. The mockery inflicted upon Jesus before the crucifixion was at the initiative of the soldiers. There is no suggestion in the Gospels that the mockery was part of the governor's 'rules of engagement'. Rather it seems as if the soldiers took it upon themselves to treat the prisoner in this way, in a way which was familiar to them from other contexts. Hugo Grotius (the Dutch lawyer and philosopher, 1583–1645) was the first scholar to notice the similarities between the treatment of Jesus and the way in which the mob of Alexandria treated Agrippa I (grandson of Herod the Great) when the king visited the city in AD 38. Agrippa was unpopular, and so the crowds mocked him by taking a well-known lunatic by the name of Karabas, decking him in mock royal finery and parading him through the streets proclaiming him king.[10] Of course, Karabas wasn't killed at the end of his play-acting, but Martial, the Roman poet and wit (c AD 38 – c AD 103), records the execution of a prisoner in the Flavian colosseum, who was forced to play the role of a brigand-king, hung from a cross, and then torn to pieces by a Scottish bear.[11] Other writers have remarked on the similarity between Jesus's treatment and the popular games of Roman Saturnalia, in which a member of every household was appointed *Saturnalicius princeps*, the lord of the feast and misrule, and was expected to exercise his rule with as much indulgence and the overturning of the normal order as possible. Our pantomimes retain a faint memory of these spectacles: men dressed as dames and women dressed as boys. The idea was the world-turned-upside-down, the weak elevated and the great ridiculed. (But of course Jesus himself preached inversion – the first shall be last and the last first / blessed are the meek / those who mourn, and so on.)

So perhaps the soldiers applied, in an unrestrained way the patterns of behaviour they had seen on stage and street-pageants. But what could be socially acceptable satire at Saturnalia, was a much more serious business at Passover. Nails, and whips, and swords will do the job when you want to kill a man: ridicule is better when you want to kill an idea. This is why Raymond Brown says: 'For neither Jew nor Roman was it enough that Jesus die; his claims have to be derided.'[12]

For the Romans, his claim to be king was sufficient cause for his death. For the Jewish authorities his claim to forgive sins demanded his death. And both ideas needed to die as well.

Christians came to understand the significance of each step Jesus took on the path to Golgotha. They realized there was a costliness in everything that Jesus suffered in the last week of his life; they realized that the experiences of his suffering were important, and attention should be properly paid to them.

In the brief period between Christianity's acceptance as a public religion in the Roman Empire and the beginning of the Persian/Arab invasions (roughly AD 313–614), it was possible for ordinary Christians to visit the places where the events of Holy Week actually took place. We have the records of seven pilgrims in the period AD 350 – AD 600 alone, as well as the excavations and building work supervised by the Empress Helena in Jerusalem, Bethlehem and the other holy places of Palestine.

However, a whole series of invasions (the Persians in AD 614, the Arabs in AD 638, and the Seljuqs in 1071) meant that travel to Palestine became fraught with danger. There were always many more Christians than there could be pilgrims, and yet the natural spiritual yearning to place oneself in the events of Holy Week remained.

To meet this need, in the later Middle Ages there grew up a series of popular devotions focused on the person of Jesus and the events of his life, of which the *Arma Christi* (see page 7) were just one expression. The Franciscans were the great innovators in this practice; from the middle of the fourteenth century the Ottoman Empire permitted them to act as custodians of the Holy Land shrines and so they knew, at first hand, the power of pilgrimage, even a 'pilgrimage of the imagination'. The genius of this inward, spiritual, journeying was Giovanni di Fidanza, St Bonaventure (1217–74), a second-generation Franciscan. His meditation, *The Tree of Life*, on the life and Passion of Christ was both influential and popular, and was translated from its original Latin into many vernacular languages. Bonaventure aimed to make a connection between his reader and the events of Christ's life, a connection that was intellectual, emotional, and imaginative. In *The Tree of Life*, there 'is a vivid application of the senses, an imaginative recreation of the Gospel scene, a drawing of the reader into the drama of the event as a witness and a participator'.[13]

Bonaventure shows this in the first line of the Prologue: this is a work in which 'With Christ I am nailed to the cross':

> The true worshipper of God and disciple of Christ,
> who desires to conform perfectly
> to the Saviour of all men,
> crucified for him,
> should, above all, strive
> with an earnest endeavour of soul
> to carry about continuously, both in his soul and
>   in his flesh,
> the cross of Christ
> until he can truly feel in himself
> what the Apostle said above.[14]

The Tree of Life is divided into three sections mapped onto the life of Christ, his pre-existence and his heavenly glorification. Within each of the three sections, Bonaventure assigns four 'fruits' (12 in all) appropriate for each section. Thus in the section 'On the Mystery of His Passion', we find 'His Confidence in Trial' (Fifth fruit), 'His Patience in Maltreatment' (Sixth fruit) and so on. The Seventh Fruit is applicable to our painting: 'His Constancy under Torture'. Bonaventure describes for his reader St John's account of the mockery, and presents a verse meditation:

Attend now,
O pride of human heart
that flees from reproach and aspires after honours!
Who is it who comes
in the likeness of the King
and yet is filled with the confusion
of a despicable slave?
He is your King and your God,
who is accounted *as a leper and the last of men*
in order to snatch you from eternal confusion
and to heal you from the disease of pride.[15]

For Bonaventure, none of the events of Jesus's life and Passion make any sense without understanding his status as the Son of God, the Incarnation of the Word. The First Fruit tells us:

Although he was great and rich, he became small and poor for us. He chose to be born away from a home in a stable, to be wrapped in swaddling clothes, to be nourished by virginal milk and to lie in a chamber between an ox and an ass. Then 'there shone upon us a day of new redemption, restoration of the past and eternal happiness. Then through-out the whole world the heavens became honey-sweet.'[16]

The Tree of Life was the source material for the para-liturgical rite (as the historians of liturgy call it) of the Stations of the Cross. Readings and prayers and movement around a parish church (at first with a varying number of stations) allowed the congregation to imagine themselves at the foot of the cross; every Christian could be a pilgrim, and stand under the gaze of the suffering Christ.

Such imaginative representations of Christ's Passion would have been familiar to Bosch. Part of the thriving cultural life of his city was expressed by amateur dramatic guilds, the chambers of rhetoric (*rederijker kamers*), which put on public entertainments during holidays and festivals. Some of these entertainments were social satires (it is thought that Bosch's painting *The Stone Operation* in which a quack doctor appears to be performing brain surgery on a foolish patient was based upon a popular comedy routine performed by the chambers). Other entertainments were religious pageants, rather like the mystery plays of English towns of the same period. The pageants were public, secular, versions of the Stations of the Cross: less reverential to be sure, but sharing in the same concern to allow their audience to make the move from *spectators* of Christ's suffering to *participants* in his Passion.

Which is why Hieronymus Bosch could properly and devoutly paint a sacred painting that showed no cross and no resurrection, and yet contained within it both Good Friday and Easter morn. The Crucifixion is depicted by the presence of the crown of thorns; the Resurrection is depicted by the seamless white robe (the *lampros*) Christ wears. Bosch includes a third biblical episode, which we see in the quizzical look Christ gives the viewer, the attention *he* pays *us*. Don't you feel that a question is being asked, the same question Jesus asked of his disciples in Caesarea Philippi: 'Who do you say that I am?' (Matthew 16.13–21 ‖ Mark 8.27–33 ‖ Luke 9.18–22). Bosch has an answer, but do we?

For we have come down to the nub and rub of the essence of Jesus: who is he, what is he, what is his relationship to the world, what is his relationship to me?

This is where that wonderful old English word 'quiddity' comes in. These days, if we hear the word used at all, it usually means some quibbling point of an argument, but when it was first used in English it meant the 'real nature or essence of a thing; that which makes a thing what it is'.[17] What is the 'quiddity' of Jesus? What is the very thing that makes him the person he is? This is the question and the point upon which all our other circling explorations of Bosch's painting come to rest.

Bosch, and those educated men and women of the late Middle Ages who viewed his painting, would see that Christ in the centre of the painting was the sublimation,[18] the essence, the perfect combination of all the political powers of the world that ever had been and ever will be, that he was the Creative Power which brought the lesser, earthly elements into existence, the *Aether* or *Quintessence* of creation, that he was the perfect person in whom all the temperaments of imperfect and imbalanced humanity were to be found in perfect, heavenly, poise.

So what can we say for ourselves and our times? I don't suppose that there are many people who would feel it necessary or persuasive to follow a 'Master of the balanced four temperaments', or to put in practice the teachings of the 'representative quintessence of the created elements'. These are not categories of thought in which we live and move and have our being: they are not *compelling*.

I think however that two themes in the quiddity of Christ speak particularly to us today. These are not new ideas about

Jesus: it is almost axiomatic that there is nothing new that can be said about him and which yet remains orthodox (there are no new heresies either: the Church has heard and refuted them all before). The two themes revolve around what we would say in answer to the question 'Who do people say that I am?' The two themes are trust and time, and we find an exploration of them in the work of three present-day artist-philosophers: Rowan Williams, Bill Viola and Brian Eno.

In *Tokens of Trust* the Archbishop of Canterbury explores what it means, in the modern, suspicious and cynical world, to say that you 'believe' in someone, or that you 'trust' them. Belief and trust in Jesus may come by seeing the way in which Jesus subverts the dominant, cultural models of belief and trust. Jesus does not force us into trusting him; although belief in him may be *compelling*, it is not *coerced*. We can see this most clearly in the scriptural witness of Jesus's relationship with his Father, with God:

> Jesus . . . isn't God just when he's being strong and in control; he's God when he speaks lovingly to God the Father, when he submerges what his human nature fears or longs for in love for the Father.[19]

We have to be careful here. We live in a culture with such clearly defined, although unconscious, ideas about human roles and relationships that language of 'love' and 'submerging' are almost inevitably marked as 'feminine' if not 'female'. Vulnerability is not a commendable or exemplary moral position. Look at the public controversy which surrounded Mark Wallinger's statue *Ecce Homo* in 1999. The first of a series of art works designed to fill the 'empty plinth' of Trafalgar Square, *Ecce Homo* is a resin and marble life-size cast of a man, naked but for a loin cloth and barbed-wire crown of thorns. The sheer puckered detail of the casting was lost however when the statue was put in position. The other statuary in the square is of heroic proportions; nine-foot-high generals and so on. The Christ being here presented to the crowds was overwhelmed by the scale of the surrounding cityscape. It must have been the artist's intention. The fragility of the bound political prisoner, in the space traditionally used in Britain for political protest and insurrection, was a very subtle undermining of our traditional reading of this episode of Jesus's trial. Very often we put the emphasis on the 'behold!': whether the blood or the heroic Son of God. Wallinger put the stress back on 'homo': this is a *man*.

People didn't like it: 'You couldn't put your faith in someone like that, he's as weak as a kitten,' said one passer-by. Another thought, 'His smallness just shows what little meaning Christianity has in the world today. He's a typically broken, lily-livered, Anglican Jesus.'[20]

This is important to understand. We do not find in Jesus (just) the moral exemplar, the good teacher, the kind person. There is a different quality to Jesus from what we have known before. His vulnerability, his smallness, his weakness, are not the same as human (feminine) vulnerability, smallness, weakness.

All of Jesus's human qualities are human qualities from which *the abuse of power has been removed*. Think about it. What would our vulnerability look like without our worries that we will be exploited by an unscrupulous 'other'? What would our loveliness look like without the sentiment that is open to manipulation? What would our smallness look like without the worry that we will be crushed by the hugeness of an indifferent world? Or better (of course), what if these worries and fears were *removed from us?* We have the answer, the Gospel says. If you want to see a human being living without the corrosive effects of the abuse of power, then look at the carpenter from Nazareth:

Jesus is divine responding embodied in our nature and our world; he responds freely and totally to the gift of the Father, and that response is no less divine than the gift— a *perfect* response that is both human and divine.[21]

But people are not *argued* into a life of faith, and Christianity is not a series of propositions to be memorized. Rather we come to know this giving and receiving, responses freely and lovingly made, not by intellectual assent, but by being in relationship. Rowan Williams calls it 'living in Jesus's company':

> Trust this, live in Jesus's company, and you will become a citizen of a new world, the world in which God's rule has arrived. You will still be living in the everyday world in which many other powers claim to be ruling; but you will have become free of them, free to co-operate or not, depending on how far they allow you to be ruled by God. And what you do and say will become a sign of what is coming. Your life will give a foretaste of God's rule . . .[22]

This relationship, an 'abiding in', is why it is sometimes helpful not to think of the 'Incarnation' (which has overtones and undertones of an impersonal process or abstract concept), but rather to think of the 'incarnated One'. It is not the process by which Jesus has entered into human existence that is important; it is the fact that *he* has.

Does this give us our first answer to the question of Jesus's quiddity, his 'whatness' for our day? Jesus is the one whom we can trust, no matter what the time of our lives or the circumstances of the world. When there is so little in our society in which we can trust, Jesus takes that role upon himself: Jesus 'has marked out the place for us all to stand'.[23]

This answer to Jesus's quiddity has to do with the *space* in which we encounter him – which naturally leads us to think about the *time* in which we might encounter him. To think about time we need the help of our other two artists, Bill Viola and Brian Eno.

Born in 1951 in New York, Bill Viola is one of the world's leading video artists, producing technologically advanced works (high-definition video, massive flat screen installations, extreme slow motion, complex sound editing) that are rooted in past expressive forms. In 2000 he was commissioned by the National Gallery to produce a work inspired by one of the Gallery's own paintings. The result was exhibited in 2003 under the title 'Bill Viola: The Passions', an exhibition which set out to explore 'the power and complexity of human emotions'.[24] High-definition, ultra-slow-motion video allows Viola and his viewers to see emotional transitions in a medium that is neither quite a painting (a fixed moment) nor a film (with an imposed linear narrative). Unlike many of his earlier works, 'The Passions' were mostly displayed without sound. This added to the 'out of time' effect: we have to manage without audible clues which we would normally, unconsciously, pick up on to identify the emotion we see; is the person laughing or crying, is it anguish or joy?

Viola denies any Christian monopoly on depictions of the Crucifixion or Resurrection. He argues that these events are representations of a primal human response to the universe. They are 'hard-wired' into the human psyche, and we can acknowledge or ignore the power of the imagery, but the power remains.[25] The work which inspired Viola was, of course, *Christ Mocked*. He said of it:

> This painting has always fascinated me. The idea of the calm centre in the chaotic, threatening circle of the world is something that I've been preoccupied with for a long time. One way that you can look at religious practice is the sense of perfecting the individual so they can stand

calmly and securely in whatever turbulent situation they might find themselves in . . . The extraordinary thing about that image is Christ staring right out of the frame towards us. He's found the only way out, right out of the picture. And who is he looking at? Us . . . he's looking right into our eyes.[26]

Viola's response to Bosch is a video panel, *The Quintet of the Astonished*. The panel is large (about 2.40 m × 1.4 m, 8 ft × 4 ½ ft). In it we see five people, from the waist up, arranged in two closely packed lines, three men at the rear, a women and a man to the front. The background is dark, the colours of their clothes are muted. At first we might think the image is still, until we tune into the slowness of the movement. Their faces are convulsed in a changing series of emotions, their hand gestures ambiguous. We cannot see what it is that is so moving them. What could be ridiculous ('luvvie' emotion in slow motion) becomes strangely compelling and affecting.

I think that *Quintet*, in its structural composition, actually owes more to another Bosch Passion scene, *Christ Carrying the Cross* in the Museum of Fine Arts in Ghent.[27] In that painting, Bosch gives us 18 faces closely packed into three rough diagonals. There is none of the circularity, none of the stillness, which we see in *Christ Mocked*. The faces in *Christ Carrying the Cross*, with the exception of Christ's and St Veronica's, are all convulsed in extreme, repellent, emotions: hatred, scorn, loathing. Although Viola's emotions are not aggressive (but it's hard to be sure that anger, or aggression, are not being expressed, given the absence of so many of the cues upon which we usually depend), because they unfold so slowly, paradoxically, there appears to be *less* movement in the video than in the painting of *Christ Carrying the Cross*. Similarly, even though there is more *expressed* emotion in *Quintet* than in *Christ Mocked* (in which the emotions are inferred), the emotional impact of the painting is greater because the object and origin of the emotions is known. The emoting *Quintet* might be affected by a massacre or by a lottery win: the origin of the emotions conditions our response to them. In *Christ Mocked* the origin of the emotions is clear: this man is about to be, unjustifiably, killed.

Viola's work is disliked by some critics for his willingness to engage with 'spiritual' themes,[28] by some for his unwillingness to engage with the physical implications of his spiritual themes,[29] and by others for the sheer amount of chronological time he expects his viewers to pay each work.[30] Even so, Viola is a fine inheritor of Bosch's exploration of the cosmic structures that undergird momentary events.

Viola uses time as a medium in his art work, as much as van Eyck and Bosch used oils. This is a resonant material for our day, for it raises important issues about the things we feel to be important. One survey has discovered that the average art gallery visitor will spend no more than 30 seconds in front of any given painting.[31] What kind of attention can be expected from the creator of a video installation which runs for 20 minutes or more? What about an art work whose running time is a thousand years? Or longer?

These questions have been explored by our third artist, Brian Eno, musician, commentator, polymath (whom we've already met on page 54 above), one of 'the pivotal figures of twentieth-century music'.[32] Eno recognizes the cultural 'attention deficit disorder' of our times and works against it. He therefore co-founded, and came up with the name for, the 'Long Now Foundation'.

The main project of the Long Now Foundation is to build a clock, but a clock with a difference. It is designed to tick once a year. It has a hand that moves once every century. Its cuckoo will appear once every thousand years, ten times in all, as the clock is designed to run for 10,000 years. It is called the Clock of the Long Now, and a prototype has been built and is on display in the Science Museum in London. It was made in time for the last Millennium; to mark the occasion, on 1 January 2000, it chimed – twice.

Why 10,000 years, and not, say, 5,000 or 100,000? 'It's because we've had technology for just about that long,' explains Alexander Rose, the executive of the Foundation. 'It's a human time scale, not a geologic or astronomical one, that makes you feel insignificant. The 10,000 years is 400 generations. You can almost imagine telling a story 400 times and having it work.'[33] Even so, 10,000 years is longer than any human institution has yet managed to survive. The longest existing businesses in the United Kingdom I know of are the Aberdeen Shore Porters' Society (established 1498), and Gill and Co, ironmongers of Oxford (established 1530): five hand movements. The Christian Church? – 20 ticks. Even the Great Pyramid of Giza has only been in existence for 5,000 years; five cuckoos.

The idea for the clock came from another founding member of the Long Now, Daniel Hillis, the computer scientist. Hillis has noted the gradual decay of 'the future':

When I was a child, people used to talk about what would happen by the year 2000. For the next thirty years they kept talking about what would happen by the year 2000, and now no one mentions a future date at all. The future has been shrinking by one year per year for my entire life.[34]

At roughly the same time that Hillis experienced the shrinking of the future, Brian Eno lived in New York City. There he experienced another, more acute, version of time and space dilation. He realized that for New York artists and musicians 'here' meant, and could only mean, 'within these four walls', and 'now' meant, and could only mean, 'the beginning of last week to the end of next week'. This domination of the Short Now and the Small Here had moral and ethical implications. Eno noticed that:

> . . . their commitment to the city was absolutely zero . . . there was no attachment to the idea of the city as a continuing entity . . . and that kind of narrowness in time-thinking slightly worried me, because it doesn't translate into terribly productive social behaviour. It doesn't encourage you to set in place projects and agreements and arrangements between people that will flower over very long periods.[35]

The example that both Eno and Hillis like to give is the hall at New College, Oxford. The roof beams were made of great oak trunks, and, 400 years after the hall was built, the beams had begun to rot away. The carpenters were able to replace them with oaks that had been planted by the college's builders for just that purpose: planning on the 400-year scale.

Of course, the implicit and explicit subject of all this thinking about time is death. Eno makes that clear when he tells the story of how he came to be interested in 'ambient music', a music which is 'as the colour of the light or the sound of the rain',[36] a music 'as ignorable as it is interesting'.[37] Waiting to catch a plane at an airport in Germany in late 1977 Eno wondered about the characteristics of the music which should be played in a modern building like that:

> I thought, 'It has to be interruptible (because there'll be announcements), it has to work outside the frequencies at which people speak, and at different speeds from speech patterns (so as not to confuse communication), and it has to be able to accommodate all the noises that

airports produce. And, most importantly for me, it has to have something to do with where you are and what you're there for – flying, floating and secretly flirting with death.' I thought, 'I want to make a kind of music that prepares you for dying – that doesn't get all bright and cheerful and pretend you're not a little apprehensive, but which makes you say to yourself, 'Actually, it's not that big a deal if I die.'[38]

Daniel Hillis also recognized the death factor in his ideas for the Clock of the Long Now. At a formal dinner he told Jonas Salk, the inventor of the polio vaccine, about the Clock project: 'Oh,' said Salk, 'you want to preserve something of yourself, just as I am preserving something of myself by having this conversation with you.'[39] Human beings are unlike every other animal species; we are aware not only of the fact of our impending death, but also the fact that who we are and what we might have become will be curtailed by death. Françoise Dastur puts it this way: 'unlike other animals, the human dies before it has exhausted all possibilities of its being'.[40] Etty Hillesum, typically, was more acute:

Living and dying, sorrow and joy, the blisters on my feet and the jasmine behind the house, the persecution and the unspeakable horrors – it is all as one in me, and I accept it all as one mighty whole . . . I wish I could live for a long time so that one day I may know how to explain it, and if I am not granted that wish, well, then somebody else will perhaps do it, carry on from where my life has been cut short. And that is why I must try to live a good and faithful life to my last breath: so that those who come after me do not have to start all over again.[41]

For Eno and Hillis a solution to the problem of death is to live in the Long Now, inhabit the Big Here, find ways to care less about death. These are goals not so very different from the traditional Christian goal of living life in the light of eternity. But there are important differences between a Long Now and Eternity.

Thinking about time and eternity is very difficult. We know this to be so because the greatest and most subtle Christian thinker, Augustine himself, said so:

> What is time? Who can explain this easily and briefly? Who can comprehend this even in thought so as to articulate the answer in words? Yet what do we speak of, in our familiar everyday conversation, more than of time . . . What then is time? Provided that no one asks me, I know. If I want to explain it to an inquirer, I do not know.[42]

The difficulty comes from the 'cloaking' that common sense gives to time. Common sense makes us think that time is one 'thing', but it should properly be thought of as possessing at least four different modes: time is multidimensional.

First there is time as *chronos*, the passage of time, what Thomas Aquinas called its 'successiveness' and Augustine 'fugitive moments': *chronos* is the form in which we mostly experience time in our lives, one damn thing after the other. *Chronos* is the time measured by clocks, and even the Clock of the Long Now will be nothing more than an elongated version of *chronos*.

The second form of time is *kairos*, time as experienced by the soul, time as the opportune moment, measured not by movement through space but by movement towards the good. *Kairos* is therefore closely related to another Greek word, *telos* (which we met on page 109 above).

Thomas Aquinas described a third measure of time, *aevum*

or *aeon*, the time of 'immaterial substances', the angels and spirits. *Aeon* has duration and the *possibility*, but not the *necessity* of change:

> . . . take angels who combine unchangeable existence with changeability of choice at the natural level, and with changeability of thoughts, affections and in their own fashion, places. These sorts of thing then are measured by the aeon, which lies somewhere between eternity and time.[43]

This doesn't seem to be very helpful for answering our double question, 'Where is wisdom to be found', and, 'Who do you say I am?' An *aeon* may give an angel all the time in the world (or indeed out of the world) to contemplate those questions, but how would we, mere mortals, experience time as *aeon*? It is impossible to imagine and impossible to comprehend.

But there is a fourth mode of time, this one without a formal Greek label, but if one is required then I suppose *tyknos* (thickness) would do. This fourth mode is not a way of measuring time, as in the previous three, but a way of experiencing time. C. S. Lewis (1898–1963) in one of his *Letters to Malcolm* says:

> I certainly believe that to be God is to enjoy an infinite present, where nothing has yet passed away and nothing is still to come. Does it follow that we can say the same of saints and angels? Or at any rate exactly the same? The dead might experience a time which is not so linear as ours – *it might, so to speak, have thickness as well as length.* Already in this life we get some thickness whenever we learn to attend to more than one thing at once. One can suppose this increased to any extent, so that though, for them as for us, the present is always becoming the past, yet each present contains unimaginably more than ours.[44]

What would 'thick time', *tyknos*, be like? How could we experience it, when we are such creatures of *chronos*? Peter Kreeft points to an imaginative description of the experience of 'thick time'.[45] In J. R. R. Tolkien's *The Lord of the Rings*, Bilbo describes his life in the house of Elrond at Rivendell:

> '. . . I make up a few songs,' said Bilbo. 'They sing them occasionally: just to please me, I think; for, of course, they aren't really good enough for Rivendell. And I listen and I think. *Time doesn't seem to pass here: it just is.* A remarkable place altogether.'[46]

Rivendell is not the only place in Middle Earth which experiences this 'is-ness' of time. When the Fellowship stay in Lothlórien, another Elvish country, they lose track of the passing of time. Sam Gamgee is surprised by the appearance of a new moon, out of its expected running. Legolas explains to him that time does not stop in Lórien:

> 'Nay, time does not tarry ever,' he said; 'but change and growth is not in all things and places alike. For the Elves the world moves, and it moves both very swift and very slow. Swift, because they themselves change little, and all else fleets by: it is a grief to them. Slow, because they do not count the running years, not for themselves. The passing seasons are but ripples ever repeated in the long long stream.'[47]

Paul Tillich (1886–1965) argued that experiencing this thickened time is the goal for humanity. He expressed the terrible contingency and transitory nature of the present:

> Is not the present moment gone when we think of it? Is not the present the ever-moving boundary line between

past and future? But a moving boundary is not a place to stand upon. If nothing were given to us except the 'no more' of the past and the 'not yet' of the future, we would not have anything. We could not speak of the time that is *our* time; we would not have 'presence'.

Our ability to have 'presence' and to find a place in which we can stand and affirm a past and a future can only come from the existence of the eternal. And more than that: it is not just the *idea* of the eternal that allows us a present presence, it is the eternal actually breaking into the present:

> Whenever we say 'now' or 'today,' we stop the flux of time for us. We accept the present and do not care that it is gone in the moment that we accept it. We live in it and it is renewed for us in every new 'present'. This is possible because every moment of time reaches into the eternal. It is the eternal that stops the flux of time for us. It is the eternal 'now' which provides for us a temporal 'now'.[48]

Tillich calls this breaking in of the eternal to the present the 'thickening' of time, the 'Eternal Now'. It is living, as the Letter to the Hebrews puts it, in the light of eternity, so as to 'exhort one another every day, as long as it is called "today", so that none of you may be hardened by the deceitfulness of sin. For we have become partners of Christ, if only we hold our first confidence firm to the end' (Hebrews 3.13–14).

We can see from this that the Eternal Now has an ethical and moral dimension to it. We become most aware of the breaking in of eternity into the succession of fugitive moments that make up our life when we attempt to 'provoke one another to love and good deeds' (Hebrews 10.24). Then we are freed to pursue 'whatever is true, whatever is honourable, whatever is just, whatever is pure, whatever is pleasing, whatever is commendable, if there is any excellence and if there is anything worthy of praise' (Philippians 4.8) so that the God of peace may be with us.

In the end the mysteries of time and space can have the same answer. To live in Jesus's company is to stand in the space he has prepared for us, and to stand in the time he has prepared for us. In Jesus's company time is thickened and space is thinned so that heaven breaks through. Matter becomes weighted with the glory of God and time is transfigured into eternity. Is this the reason why in Bosch's painting Christ's robe is both white (bright with the glory of heaven) and so very thinly painted (so thin, that the preparatory drawings of the artist are visible underneath)? Is Bosch showing us the effulgence of eternity at its thickest point in our world of space and time, in the person of the Way, the Truth and the Light?

So, to return to the dilemma of Lu Tze: is wisdom found far away or very near? Do we seek proximate enlightenment or perplexity elsewhere? The answer has to be both:

> Where can I go from your spirit?
>   Or where can I flee from your presence?
> If I ascend to heaven, you are there;
>   if I make my bed in Sheol, you are there.
> If I take the wings of the morning
>   and settle at the farthest limits of the sea,
> even there your hand shall lead me,
>   and your right hand shall hold me fast.
>
> (Psalm 139.7–10)

This is the insight of the psalmist: there is nowhere in creation off-limits to the operation of God's loving wisdom, for without that wisdom creation itself could not be sustained.

'Who do you say that I am?' We can find the answer in the

briefest heartbeat, and in the unimaginable years of the Long Now. We can find the answer within the confines of our room, in prayer and meditation, and in the outermost reaches of the universe, through our observatories and satellites. We can find the answer in the face and character of our neighbours and in the darkest corners of our own psyches. We can find the answer in the whirling circles of our lives, and in the poised stillness of depictions of Christ. We can find the answer even in the asking of the question, 'Who do you say that I am?' To hear Christ ask the question of us is to begin to find the answer in the whole of our lives. The question is the heart of all; the rest is commentary.

Notes

1 Terry Pratchett, *The Thief of Time* (London: Doubleday, 2001), p. 28, p. 70, p. 93.

2 Norman Cantor, *Inventing the Middle Ages: The lives, works, and ideas of the great medievalists of the twentieth century* (New York: William Morrow, 1991) , p. 414.

3 Peter Walker, 'Pilgrimage in the Early Church' in Craig Bartholomew and Fred Hughes, eds, *Explorations in a Christian theology of pilgrimage* (Aldershot: Ashgate, 2003), p. 84.

4 Raymond Brown, *The Death of the Messiah : From Gethsemane to the Grave, a Commentary on the Passion Narratives in the Four Gospels* (New York: Doubleday, 1994), Vol. 1, p. 568, n. 1.

5 Ibid., Table 2, pp. 570–1.

6 Josephus, *The Jewish War* (II 301–8), translated by G.A. Williamson, 2nd edition (London: Penguin, 1981), pp. 151ff.

7 See Haim Cohn, *The Trial and Death of Jesus* (London: Weidenfeld and Nicholson, 1972) pp. 171–3.

8 'Swiss man jailed for Thai insult', BBC News Online, 29 March 2007 http://news.bbc.co.uk/1/hi/world/asia-pacific/6505237.stm (accessed 6 April 2008).

9 Cohn, *Trial*, p. 173.

10 We have an account of this in the writings of the Jewish-Greek philosopher Philo: *Flaccus* 6. See Paul Winter, *On the Trial of Jesus*, 2nd edition (Berlin: Walter de Gruyter, 1974), pp. 147–8.

11 Martial, *Liber spectaculorum* 7. See Kathleen M. Coleman, trans., in

Martial: Liber Spectaculorum (Oxford: OUP, 2006), p. 82.

12 Raymond Brown, *A Crucified Christ in Holy Week* (Collegeville, MN: The Liturgical Press, 1986), p. 29.

13 Ewert Cousins, introduction to *Bonaventure: The Soul's Journey into Life, The Tree of Life, The Life of St Francis* (Classics of Western Spirituality Series) (London: SPCK, 1978) p. 35.

14 In other words, Galatians 2.19. Bonaventure, 'Prologue to the Tree of Life', §1 in Ewert Cousins, trans., *Bonaventure*, p. 119.

15 Bonaventure, 'Seventh Fruit', §25 in Ewert Cousins, *Bonaventure*, pp. 147–8. Italics are a quotation from Vulgate Isaiah 53:4,3.

16 Bonaventure, 'First Fruit', §4 in Ewert Cousins, *Bonaventure*, p. 128. The quotation is from the Roman Breviary for Nocturne on Christmas Day.

17 'Quiddity', *Oxford English Dictionary*, 2nd edition (Oxford: OUP, 1989).

18 A word with its origins in alchemy and chemical science, but which has also been taken up in psychology as well: a truly Boschian connectedness of concepts!

19 Rowan Williams, *Tokens of Trust: An introduction to Christian belief* (Norwich: Canterbury Press, 2007), p. 66.

20 Fiachra Gibbons, 'Behold Jesus, just another ordinary bloke', *The Guardian*, 22 July 1999. Available online from www.guardian.co.uk/religion/Story/0,2763,205091,00.html (accessed 6 April 2008).

21 Williams, *Tokens of Trust*, p. 66.

22 Ibid., p. 58.

23 Ibid., p. 61.

24 'Bill Viola: 'The Passions', The National Gallery, London. See the online exhibition at www.nationalgallery.org.uk/exhibitions/bill_viola (accessed 6 April 2008).

25 See the interview in the short film *Bill Viola and Emergence*, by Mark Kidel, streamed from the Getty Museum's website. Available online from www.getty.edu/art/exhibitions/viola/exhibition.html (accessed 6 April 2008).

26 Bill Viola, *The Quintet of the Astonished: Influences from Past Art*, on the National Gallery exhibition's website.

27 Online exhibition, in English, available online from www.mskgent.be (accessed 6 April 2008).

28 See Adrian Searle's dyspeptic review 'Losing my religion: Bill Violas startling, fascinating videos are like paintings that move' in G2 Arts, *The Guardian*, 23 October 2003.

29 Tom Lubbock, 'Passionless Moments', *The Independent*, 21 October 2003: 'The work tries to avert its gaze from the prosaic facts of the matter. It's vital that you see these figures as existing in an ethereal dimension, in a realm of pure feeling . . . In Viola-land, we are all souls.'

30 Philip Hensher, 'Videos that don't move', *The Mail on Sunday*, 9 November 2003: video art, all too often, means 'looking at TV sets while a crummily filmed face talks interminably about their love life or whatever'.

31 Doris Lockhart Saatchi '"Close-up and personal": A profile of Bill Viola', *The Independent*, 10 October 2003.

32 Mark Prendergast, *The Ambient Century: From Mahler to Moby – the evolution of sound in the electronic age*, 2nd edition (London: Bloomsbury, 2003), p. 115.

33 Quoted in Peter Hartlaub, 'The March of Time', *The San Francisco Chronicle*, 30 July 2006.

34 Daniel Hillis, quoted in Stewart Brand, *The Clock and Library Projects*, on the website of the Long Now Foundation, www.longnow.org/about (accessed 6 April 2008).

35 Brian Eno, 'The Long Now', transcript of a talk given as part of the Long Now Foundation's series of *Seminars About Long Term Thinking*, Fort Mason, San Francisco, 14 November, 2003. Available online from www.enoshop.co.uk (accessed 6 April 2008).

36 Eno's definition, quoted in Prendergast, p. 115.

37 Eno's definition, in the liner notes for *Ambient 1: Music for Airports* (editions EG, EGS 201, 1978).

38 Brian Eno, 'Ambient Music', in *A Year with Swollen Appendices: Brian Eno's Diary* (London: Faber and Faber, 1996), p. 295. Curiously, Eno tells the story in a very different way in other places. In another version he notices the music that is actually already playing in the airport, and its frantic insistence on *not* thinking about death: '. . . the message . . . is "don't worry you're not going to die" – music that is deliberately very lightweight, with no threat, where everything's got a nice smile'. The problem, of course, for muzak with that particular message is that you realize 'all they're saying to you is "Death? Don't mention it! Don't even think about it" . . . So I started thinking "What would make you not think about death so much?" and I started to think that what you really needed in airports was the kind of music that would make you care less about your own life, that would make you not be so concerned about the prospect of dying.'

(Brian Eno, 'The Long Now').

39 Daniel Hillis, 'The 10,000 Year Clock', available online from www.longnow.org/projects/clock (accessed 6 April 2008).

40 Françoise Dastur, 'Death: an essay on finitude' (1996), quoted in Hayden Ramsay, 'Death Part II: The significance of our deaths' in *New Blackfriars*, Vol. 86/1003 (May 2005), p. 303.

41 Etty Hillesum, diary entry for 3 July 1942 in *An Interrupted Life: The Diaries and Letters of Etty Hillesum, 1941–43*, translated by Arnold Pomerans (London: Persephone Books, 1999), pp. 188–9.

42 Augustine, *Confessions*, XI.14, translated by Henry Chadwick (Oxford; New York: OUP, 1991), p. 230.

43 Thomas Aquinas, *Summa Theologiae*, I.x.5, in Timothy McDermott, ed. and trans. (London: Eyre & Spottiswoode for Blackfriars, 1964–81), Vol. 2, pp. 149–51.

44 C. S. Lewis, Letter 20 in *Letters to Malcolm: Chiefly on Prayer* (London: Geoffrey Bles, 1964) p. 141. Emphasis added.

45 Peter Kreeft, 'Time and Eternity', a talk delivered to the C. S. Lewis Foundation Summer Institute, Oxford, July 2002. Available online from www.peterkreeft.com/audio/20_cslewis_time-eternity.htm (accessed 6 April 2008).

46 J. R. R. Tolkien, *The Lord of the Rings: The Fellowship of the Ring*, Book II, Chapter 1, 'Many Meetings' (London: HarperCollins, 1991/1954), p. 247. Emphasis added.

47 Ibid., Ch. IX, 'The Great River', pp. 408–9.

48 Paul Tillich, *The Eternal Now: Sermons* (London: SCM Press, 1963), pp. 110f. Emphasis in the original.

A Certain Regard

I began my journey with Bosch many years ago. When I first saw the painting I was attracted to it because it was by the master of the great, proto-surrealist triptychs *The Hay Wain* and *The Garden of Earthly Delights*. I stayed in front of the painting, long after the trickeries of surrealism bored me, because I found something compelling and mysterious in its simplicity. The apparent straightforwardness of its composition, the people depicted, their dress and posture, gradually began to get under my skin. I slowly realized there was very little straightforward about this painting. I didn't know that what had once seemed straight would turn into a succession of circles that would take me 25 years to orbit and untangle.

As I began the journey around the painting I discovered that I would have to immerse myself, as far as possible, in the mental and cultural world of early sixteenth-century Europe. Bosch made certain assumptions to convey the meaning of the painting, and if I didn't begin to comprehend, in whatever partial way, those assumptions then I would never grasp its meaning. At first I thought comprehension would involve surrendering something of my own mental and cultural world. As I lived in a post-Reformation, post-Enlightenment, post-Einsteinian, post-Freudian world, I would have to pretend to 'forget' some of the knowledge that my time and culture had acquired in the 500 years since Bosch lived in order to understand his 'primitive' world.

I quickly realized that this was post-Reformation, post-Enlightenment hubris. In order to understand Bosch, I didn't need to pretend to be less educated. I needed to become *more* educated: to become comfortable in categories of thought and knowledge which my post-post world had surrendered or forgotten or rejected. It was as I began to learn this forgotten knowledge that I really began to appreciate the depth and sophistication of the world in which Bosch worked, the paradigm that he painted.

Which is why this book seems to have wandered through so many by-ways and apparent cul-de-sacs: alchemy, astrology, elemental science, sixteenth-century geopolitics and fifteenth-century religious disciplines. Bosch lived at the centre of multiple networks of knowledge: understanding these networks or matrices helped me to circle the painting, and to (begin to) comprehend it. Which leaves me . . . where?

I still stand in front of the painting and find myself unsettled by the simplicity of the vision with which Bosch presents me.

I find myself questioned, in all the political, scientific, moral and spiritual conventions by which I choose to mark out my life.

I find myself made complicit in the tormenting of a single man hundreds of years ago.

I find myself taking the part, one after the other, of each of the tormentors, matching myself upon their role and actions, and savouring the cruelty that it allows me to indulge in: like running my tongue around a broken tooth, there is something deliciously painful in imagining being quite so uninhibited in a demonstration of human wickedness.

And yet, and yet, most of all, no matter how much I look at the painting, it is the gaze out of the painting — the eyes around which both the whole composition and the whole cosmos of the painting circle — which is the active agent in this relationship. I am more looked upon than looking.

I described my first impressions of the painting under the title 'An unrelenting gaze', and there is something unrelenting about the gaze that Bosch has given Christ. But I realize now that 'unrelenting' is too harsh a word, for it implies seeing without compassion, viewing without forgiveness. Everything that I have learnt about the political, scientific, moral and spiritual world of Bosch and his painting, and everything I have learnt about God and Jesus Christ through the painting, shows me that there is no such thing as Christ without compassion, without forgiveness. Instead now, when I feel myself to be pinned by the look coming from the wounded and suffering man at the centre of the painting, I think instead that it is *a certain regard*: 'certain' because it is *this* regard – specific, rooted in a time and place and a person; 'certain' also because it is sure, and reliable and trustworthy – this is a look that will never waver as all else that is created will waver. It is a 'regard' for all its senses of looking at, taking notice, giving heed to, and especially taking account of. Christ is looking at me in the moment of his great suffering, not to condemn me but to show me that, even in the moment of his great suffering, I am something and someone who is worthy of his attention: 'This is being accomplished for you.'

Recall, for a moment, the occasions in the Gospels in which Jesus is recorded as having 'looked upon' someone. What happens in these records? Think of the moment alluded to in Bosch's painting, when Jesus looks upon Peter at the moment of Peter's betrayal:

Then about an hour later yet another kept insisting, 'Surely this man also was with him; for he is a Galilean.' But Peter said, 'Man, I do not know what you are talking about!' At that moment, while he was still speaking, the cock crowed. The Lord turned and looked at Peter. Then Peter remembered the word of the Lord, how he had said to him, 'Before the cock crows today, you will deny me three times.' And he went out and wept bitterly. (Luke 22.59–62 ‖ Mark 14.66–72 ‖ Matthew 26.69–75)

Here, Jesus's look is the moment of Peter's judgement, a judgement which provokes an existential crisis in the disciple: he 'goes out', just as Judas 'goes out' from the Last Supper. But whereas Judas goes out into the darkness to do Satan's will (John 13.27–30) and ultimately finds damnation, Peter goes out to learn the full implications of his confession at Caesarea Philippi, 'You are the Messiah', and his understanding of Jesus's status as Messiah after the feeding of the 5,000:

So Jesus asked the twelve, 'Do you also wish to go away?' Simon Peter answered him, 'Lord, to whom can we go? You have the words of eternal life. We have come to believe and know that you are the Holy One of God.' (John 6.67–69)

Peter realizes that there is nowhere else and no one else to go to: he leaves the (now threatening) light of the fireside in the high priest's house, and he goes out, not into the darkness of Judas's damnation, but into darkness where Christ is already to be found. Dorothy Sayer's poem 'The Gates of Paradise' beautifully expresses an encounter with Christ in the darkness of hell's most powerful night. The poem tells of the journey that Judas makes in the hours after his death, across a lone and drear desert. He meets the two thieves who died alongside Christ, but when they learn who he is and of what he is guilty, they refuse to accompany him. Eventually he encounters a grey-hooded man who agrees to walk with him to the gates of Hades and beyond.

The second robber went his way,
And Judas walked alone,
Till he was aware of a grey man,
That sat upon a stone,
And the lamp he had in his right hand
Shone brighter than the moon.
'Come hither, come hither, thou darkling man,
And bear me company,
This lamp I hold will give us light,
Enough for thee and me.'

When the two reach Hell's gates and are greeted by Satan, the grey-hooded man is revealed to be Jesus.

Satan looked out from Hades gate,
His hand upon the key,
'Good souls, before I let you in, First tell me who ye be.'
'We be two men that died of late
And come to keep Hell's tryst,
This is Judas Iscariot,
And I am Jesus Christ.'[1]

Here is the Jesus of the certain regard. Think also of the healing miracles recorded in Luke's Gospel. In the healing of the crippled woman (Luke 13.10–17), Luke tells us that the moment of her healing is not when Jesus prays to heaven, or lays hands on her, but, simply, when Jesus looks upon her, and says, 'Woman, you are set free from your ailment.' There is no condemnation in his gaze, but a trust and a knowledge that is greater and more compassionate than any other's.

Finally, think of another encounter, one as Christ is hung upon the cross, and the moment of his death comes nearer. He sees the crowds, still mocking him and tormenting him, and he looks upon them with a prayer: 'Father, forgive them;

for they do not know what they are doing' (Luke 23.34). Even in a moment, which could properly hold judgement for the perverse persecution of God's chosen one, the chosen one himself prays for forgiveness, a prayer and a forgiveness which follows his seeing and his knowledge of his persecutors.

In all these encounters, when Christ looks upon the sinful and hurting people of God's creation, he is filled with compassion. His words are of forgiveness and comfort, and his gaze is that of love. It is this look of love that Bosch conveys so completely in his painting.

So, at the end of all this circling, what am I compelled to say about the question that I brought on the journey: what can Bosch teach me about being human?

First, to be a human being means involvement with other human beings. We are most human – *I* am most human – when we are in community: homo sapiens is truly *homo politicus*. To be fully human, I need to be fully engaged with my community. But communities are made up of individually fallen and sinful men and women, and communities themselves may come to be fallen and sinful, *structurally* turning people away from the possibility of living the most humanly full lives. *Homo politicus* therefore should be critically engaged with community, prepared to affirm those actions and attitudes of the community which are of God as well as those actions and attitudes of the community which speak of the rulers and powers of this world: 'in the world but not of the world', as John the Evangelist defined it. So, we can see in Bosch's painting a properly critical attitude to the secular and religious powers of his day, and we can affirm his critique. We can also see, though, a suspicious, slanderous depiction of those groups which Bosch thought threatened his society: Jews and Muslims. We condemn those depictions, even though we might recognize the contingent reasons why Bosch might have thought the way he did.

Second, I must remember that to be a human being requires me to exercise the full range of gifts and talents and skills given me by the creator God. Supreme among those gifts is reason, allied with humanity's insatiable curiosity about the natural world. As God is reasonable, so too is His creation. We share in His rational nature and therefore attempting to understand creation through the exercise of my reason is an expression of my fundamental nature. I should never allow others, who do not comprehend this insight, to draw up childish rules which delimit the exercise of my reason, like 'religious people are not reasonable, so cannot be scientists' or 'religion hates science and science hates religion'. These beliefs, so deep and so broad in our culture, are not part of either Bosch's world nor the fullness of a Christian understanding of the world. (Fundamentalists who unwittingly collaborate with the so-called 'rationalists' in setting up these divisions between faith and reason should be similarly resisted.) To be human is to be rational, and to apply that rationality to the getting of knowledge.

Third, I must remember that to be a human being is to experience the gifts of emotion. We are like icebergs, with many layers of needs and feelings and impulses concealed beneath the surface of the public persona we choose to present to the world and to ourselves. I should be aware of study and insights from psychologists on the healthy development of human happiness, and how those studies relate to my personal situation. And then I should allow myself to be changed, letting go of the things that prevent me from becoming the fully integrated human being as represented by Jesus in the centre of Bosch's painting.

Fourth, I take away from Bosch's inhabitation of the milieu of the Brethren of the Common Life, and the genius of religious discipline which the IJssel valley seemed to inculcate, the need for the spiritual discipline: practice in the presence of

God, and the insights and assistance that the breadth of the Church's tradition can provide me. The 're-monking' of the Church is something that needs to happen on an individual level as well as an institutional level: I need to be re-monked, in my time and place. And, remembering the example of Etty Hillesum, I should never think that these disciplines are to be followed in quiet repose, when the world treats me with kindness and peace. Etty shows that learning how to kneel, letting the circle break the plane of the painting, is something that is best done, most urgently undertaken, in times of tumult and toil.

Fifth, I should allow my whole life to be centred on Jesus in the light of eternity. He is one that I can fully trust; completely and wholly. In the trusting, in the surrendering of myself to him, I will find myself renewed, remade and returned to myself. And when I find myself so changed and transformed, more myself than I could ever imagine, I will find myself standing in the presence of Christ and the glory of the Father, and all will be well. I will be at the very centre of the circles, all the whirling circles of creation, and in that still place I will rejoice.

'God's glory is man made fully alive and man is fully alive when he beholds God.'[2] A Father of the Church taught that. Bosch painted that. Now it is my task and calling to live it.

Notes
1   Dorothy L. Sayers, 'The Gates of Paradise', from *Opus 1* (Oxford: B. H. Blackwell, 1916).
2   Irenaeus, in *Adversus haereses* ('Against Heresies') (c AD 175–185); 4.20.7.

Appendix:
Who Was Hieronymous Bosch?

We have spent so much time in the company of one of his greatest works, and explored something of the political, scientific religious and cultural background of his day, and yet Bosch remains a shadowy figure. Perhaps it would be helpful to set out what we know about the artist.

Carl Jung called him the master of the monstrous,[1] although we don't see much that is monstrous in this example of his work. Or, at least, what is monstrous is also completely human.

Jeroen van Aken was born to a family of painters in the prosperous city of 's-Hertogenbosch (also known as Bois-le-duc or Den Bosch) in the Duchy of Brabant. The duchy straddled the borders of modern-day Netherlands and Belgium, and the city of the van Akens lay just to the north of the present border. Brabant, then and now, was a border place, with a fluid population. The van Akens themselves show evidence of this; historians believe the family name came from Aachen, in the Rhineland (van Aken: 'from Aachen'). During Jeroen's lifetime his hometown exploded in size. In four years, from 1496 to 1500, the city grew from 17,280 to 25,000 inhabitants. A border city could always enjoy the profits of trade, and 's-Hertogenbosch made the most of its position between the lands belonging to the barony of Breda and the Duchy of Brabant, and its proximity to the trading routes of the North Sea. The cloth trade was especially important, and the city was famous for its metal workers, organ builders and agricultural markets. The city museum in 's-Hertogenbosch holds a painting of market day in the city square. Painted in about 1530 it shows rows of neatly tented booths, filled with bolts of dyed cloth: reds are very popular. The Ashmolean Museum in Oxford has a beautifully delicate watercolour by Antonius van den Wyngaerde of 's-Hertogenbosch set in its surrounding countryside. It is a tidy, prosperous world. The city walls are tall and in good repair, the windmills are dotted in the well-tended fields, and the cathedral of St John stands proudly over the neat houses.

The city was famous for its learning as well; a Latin school had been long established and the great Dutch humanist Desiderius Erasmus was a pupil at the school in the mid-1480s. A printing press began business in 1484, only 30 years after being invented by Johannes Gutenberg in Mainz. In the late fifteenth century, learning went with piety. Perhaps one in 20 of the population in Jeroen's lifetime were members of one religious order or another. The Franciscans, whose founder St Francis was the patron saint of weavers, were present in the city from the early 1230s. The Dominican friars, whose vocation was first to learning, and then the expounding of the Gospel to the masses, were to present, as well as a number of religious houses for women, hospitals for the infirm, hospices for travellers. There was a Charterhouse, a Carthusian monastery in which the monks lived solitary lives, in austerity and silent prayer. There were at least 50 monasteries, friaries and churches in and around 's-Hertogenbosch. Two of the houses belonged, as we have learnt, to the lay religious order the Brothers and Sisters of the Common Life. Albertus Cuperinus, a monk from 's-Hertogenbosch who published a chronicle of the city in 1557, called his home town a 'pious and pleasant city' – so pious, in fact, that by 1526, ten years after Bosch's death, one in 19 of the population were members of one religious order or another.[2]

The piety and pleasantry did not continue, though. In the century and a half after Jeroen's death religious wars swept through Europe, and the Spanish Netherlands were a battleground. Churches were burned, monasteries sacked and records destroyed. Perhaps this is one reason why there is such a small paper trail for our painter. Perhaps another reason for the poverty of the historical record is that Jeroen lived in the last generation before the lives of the painters became interesting and important in themselves. The first great biographer of artists was Giorgio Vasari (1511–1574). His book *The Lives of the Artists* was published in 1550 and concentrated on the artists known to that most fantastically self-regarding society, Renaissance Italy. The sophisticated Romans and Florentines and Pisans wanted to know about the geniuses who had worked in their midst, not in the artisans of some cold grey town in the north. The first Dutch art historian, Karel van Mander, did not publish his *Book of Painters* until 1604. By then Jeroen's style was no longer in fashion, and his works had been dispersed throughout Europe.

So we have very little in the way of written evidence, but in the 60 years since the (presumed) 500th anniversary of Jeroen's birth, skilled historians have combed the archives that do remain, and have managed to trace at least the outline of his life.

The records suggest that Jeroen was born in or around 1450. His grandfather had been a painter in Nijmegen; it was he who moved to 's-Hertogenbosch, perhaps to take part in the building of St John's Church. Jeroen's father, Antonius, was one of five sons, all of whom were painters. It is important that we don't think of the van Aken dynasty as being a family of 'artists' if by that we mean an idea of the independent creator of a commodity called 'art', pursuing a creative muse to the exclusion of all other practical matters. In the fifteenth century, painters were craftsmen, often of great skill and vision to be sure, but men who painted to order. It was a trade and painters learnt their skills as apprentices in workshops overseen by the 'Master Painter', the one whose skill, learning and commercial success allowed him the title, granted by the guild of painters. Jeroen, and his brother Goessens, began their working lives as apprentices of this type in the family studio, a large stone house on the market place.

By 1474 Bosch had reached his legal maturity: in that year, an account book shows him acting in a property transaction on behalf of his sister. In 1480 he is referred to as *Jeroen di maelre*, Jerome the painter. In 1481 he married Aleyt Goyarts van den Meervenne. Many historians have argued that Aleyt was a much older woman than Jeroen, and came from a family of much higher status: it is only after his marriage that Jeroen begins to appear regularly in the property register. Aleyt gave him the money to speculate and to paint whatever he wanted. It was the freedom from the need to conform to the wishes of patrons that allowed Jeroen to develop his unique style. Perhaps. Against this must be set the fact that Bosch's marriage lasted 36 years, and Aleyt outlived her husband for seven. If she had been much older than the 25- to 30-year-old Bosch at their marriage, then she must have lived into her 90s! Another possible explanation is that historians have confused Bosch's wife with his mother, who bore the similar name of Aleyt van der Mynnen.

Jeroen van Aken did not sign all his paintings and dated none of them. Those he did sign vary in the name he put to them: 'Jheronimus' or 'Jeronimus' or, most commonly, his Dutch name and the town of his birth in Latin: Hieronymus Bosch. The grand Latin name matched the success of his career. The tax rolls of the early sixteenth century show that Bosch was in the top 10 per cent of the wealthy: three years before his death he was in the top 6 per cent.[3] Life was good.

With wealth and status came responsibility, and one way we

know in which Bosch expressed his responsibilities was his membership of the Brotherhood of Our Lady (*Illustere Lieve-Vrouwe-Broederschap*), founded in 's-Hertogenbosch in 1318. The Brotherhood was a little like the 'friendly societies' of our day, the Freemasons or the Soroptimists; its members were obliged to provide support for each other in times of hardship or need, to perform acts of charity. The pattern for this charity were the acts of mercy described in Matthew 25. Those who wish to be counted righteous by the Son of Man should recognize that works of kindness performed for the imprisoned, the naked, the thirsty, the homeless, are works of kindness performed to the Son of Man himself.

As well as providing a vital welfare function in a society without social security, the Brotherhood also worked as the 'glue' that cemented together an expanding, changing city. It was so successful in what it set out to do, that by Bosch's day it was one of the most important confraternities in northern Europe. In Bosch's lifetime, the Brotherhood had paid for and built a confraternity chapel in the parish church of St John, which only became a cathedral 70 years after Bosch's death. Built in the latest, 'advanced', Gothic style, it was originally decorated with richly painted frescoes. The Brotherhood also maintained the shrine to Our Lady in the cathedral, and paid musicians to sing in the daily offices. The Brotherhood's house was just across the city square from their chapel, and the life of the Brotherhood was centred on these two buildings, in prayer and table fellowship. Every member was obliged to provide hospitality for his brothers, opportunities for what we would call 'networking'. The banquets were expressions of lavish generosity, at which expensive gifts were exchanged. It cost a lot to be a senior member of the Brotherhood. Bosch is recorded as having become a sworn member in 1488, after which he is referred to as a 'cleric', a lay rank rather than an ecclesiastical one.

Membership ranged over the breadth of Dutch society: men and women, aristocrats and artisans. It was a vital thread in the fabric of Dutch society.

These important lay organizations furnished essential personal, familial, religious, economic and political advantages, all of which directly increased the status and merits of members during their lives and ensured a shortened stay in purgatory after death.[4]

Of course, there were dangers in being a member of such a Brotherhood, dangers to one's immortal soul. It might be easy for elaborate dinners and entertainments to become the be all and end all, for the networking to outshine the acts of mercy. Anthony Trollope, from a very different time and culture, satirized in *The Warden* (the first of his Barchester Chronicles) the charity that spent more on its trustees than it did on its beneficiaries.[5]

Perhaps this was the particular situation which lay behind the general lesson and accusation of Bosch's triptych *The Hay Wain*. An army of sinful, greedy people gather around a hay cart, whose load symbolizes the passing nature of the wealth of this world: 'the grass of the field, which is alive today and tomorrow is thrown into the oven' (Luke 12.28, which immediately follows, of course, the Parable of the Rich Fool in Luke 12.16–21). Each attempts to grab what he can, with no regard for the needs of others. No one in society is exempt: a fat monk organizes four nuns to fill bags for him, and riding behind are the aristocrats, princes of Church and state. Everyone is susceptible to the sin of gluttony, which leads to the greater sin of forgetting our neighbours.

Even so, it was his membership of the Brotherhood which tells us of the end of Bosch's life. An account book records a funeral Mass held for Bosch on 8 August 1516, and a meal held in memory of him the same year. He had lived and worked for his entire life in the same small town.

But the Brotherhood of Our Lady was the means by which Bosch's work was opened to wider European society. The Counts of Nassau, sworn into the Brotherhood, once owned the triptych *The Garden of Earthly Delights*. Diego de Guevara, a Spanish nobleman, owned six paintings by Bosch. The Spanish connection led him to the royal family: Philip the Handsome, son of the Holy Roman Emperor Maximilian I, owned a *Last Judgement*, and Isabella of Spain, at her death in 1504, had three pictures by Bosch. After Bosch's own death, Philip II of Spain (husband of Mary Tudor and enemy of Elizabeth I) kept *The Seven Deadly Sins and Four Last Things* in his bedroom in the Escorial Palace in Madrid. The artisan from an obscure part of the Lowlands had entered international society.

The Spanish taste for Bosch's work is the reason why so many of his great works are to be found in the galleries of the former Holy Roman Empire which, in Bosch's day and for a hundred years after, was ruled by the Spanish branch of the Habsburg family. It is in the Prado, the royal gallery of Madrid, where we find three of Bosch's greatest masterpieces: *The Hay Wain*, *The Adoration of the Magi*, and *The Garden of Earthly Delights*. It is this last painting that is Bosch's most famous work, and the one which defines, for most people, his style and viewpoint.

The three Prado works are triptychs, paintings on three panels, which are connected physically and thematically. There is a central panel, flanked by two outer panels, which are hinged to form a door that can be closed over the central panel. The artist could paint, if he wished, on five separate panels, and sometimes on a sixth, the rear of the central panel, if the triptych was fixed to a free-standing altar. Usually the inside of the triptych was the more important subject, and the central panel the most important of all. The artist would show this hierarchy of importance by his choice of subject matter and technique. Often, in Bosch's day, artists painted the outside panels, visible only when the triptych was closed, using a grisaille method, painting in shades of grey, or some other neutral colour, imitating the effect of sculpture. The subjects would include sharply depicted shadows, so that the closed triptych would look like part of the built environment of the church. We can see an example of this technique by Bosch in the outer panels of the Vienna *Last Judgement*: St James the Great, and St Bavo (the patron saint of Ghent), are depicted in a palette of greys and muted buff.

Inside the triptych different rules applied. Here the artist could use the full colour palette and, whereas the outside was muted, the inside should be spectacular. The effect of opening a triptych must have been like the move from black and white Kansas to Technicolor Oz in *The Wizard of Oz*. This was a different world, the true world, the real world, that you could now look upon.

Bosch painted in a style that is recognizably related to other artists of what is called the 'Northern Renaissance', men such as van Eyck and van der Weyden. Like them, Bosch worked on wooden panels, using the new medium of oil paints, with mineral pigments suspended in oil[6] (southern European artists continued to prefer using colours suspended in egg tempera). The wooden board would be prepared with a mixture of chalk and glue – in the south it was usually the mixture of plaster and glue known as gesso (modern-day art science can test for the difference between calcium carbonate, that is, chalk, and calcium sulphate, that is, gesso).[7] Next came the underdrawing, the sketching out of the composition. Van Eyck was unusual in the detail and fullness of his underdrawing: often he would block out shadows and background details. Bosch, like Roger van der Weyden, was sketchier and more spontaneous; examination of underdrawings using IRR (infrared reflectography) shows that changes were often made in the composition. After the underdrawing a thin layer of paint, the underpainting (called *doodverw*, 'dead colour', in Dutch) usually flesh-coloured or grey, would be applied; thin enough to show the under-drawing, thick enough to prevent the rest of the paint layers from being absorbed. The other Netherlandish artists would build up the painting in layer after layer of finely applied colours, producing paintings that shine like jewels. Each colour would consist of three or four layers, with the lightest painted first, as they were the least transparent. Light could penetrate the layers and would be reflected by the underpainting and the ground. Bosch, on the other hand, seemed to have worked much more rapidly, allowing the paints that he applied to the prepared surface of his panel to be thin enough for the under-coat to show through. Van Mander, in his history of Dutch artists, says this of Bosch's technique:

> . . . a sure, rapid, and appealing style, executing many objects directly on the panel . . . a manner of sketching and drawing directly on the white ground of the panel and layering over them a transparent, flesh-coloured prime coat, and he often allowed the undercoats to contribute to the total effect.[8]

Bosch shared with the other artists of the Northern Renaissance a new way of approaching painting. For them paintings were to be read like texts, to be packed full of meaning: they were never to be wallpaper. Erwin Panofsky thought this style of painting deserved its own name: *Ars nova* he called it, the 'new style': 'precious or tortured sentiment gave way to simple, strong and uninhibited veracity . . . colouristic and luminary values [were thought of] . . . as primary rather than secondary factors of pictorial composition'[9]

Sharing in the developing scientific understanding of the world, the painters of the Northern Renaissance believed that nature could also be read for meaning. They became concerned to depict natural subjects naturally. In *ars nova* everything represents a deeper truth, and so everything is worthy of being depicted as accurately as possible. This is particularly true of Bosch's use of nature, perspective and space. As Laurinda Dixon describes it, Bosch portrays 'natural forms less distinctly as they recede in spatial registers, culminating in filmy atmospheric vistas of converging water and sky'.[10]

In other words, Bosch was able to add depth to his paintings by varying his colour palette and the manner of applying the colour. By adding *depth*, he added *mystery*.

The most clear-cut and notorious example of the marrying of symbolic paintings and *ars nova* techniques is found in Bosch's most famous work, *The Garden of Earthly Delights*. Here Bosch presents the contrast between outside and inside, between the world as we perceive it, and the world into which God calls us.

The *Garden* is a triptych, of enormous size. The outside closed panels show one subject, divided into two. It is the creation of the world, painted as a sectioned transparent globe, hovering in the vastness of space, but containing all that was known to human science. In the top left of the panels is God the Father, the old man on the clouds, crowned as Lord and Creator of the Universe. Painted in Latin are two verses from Genesis: 'For He spoke, and it was', 'By His command, they were created.' When we open the panels, we see what was created.

It is an assault on our visual senses: three panels, each 2¼ metres high, painted in greens, blues, lustrous pinks, and darkest blacks. At first glance, the three panels seem to be simple enough to interpret: at the left, the garden of Eden, with Adam and Eve, pure in their pre-fall nakedness, being joined together by God, in the appearance of Christ. Above them is a pink fountain, that suggests, in its shape, both succulent plants and crab-like claws. Beneath the feet of the first humans, strange, flippered, beaked and winged creatures emerge from a primeval swamp.

Often the central panel is described as showing the children of Adam and Eve living the life, and making the choices, that will eventually lead them to the perdition depicted in the right-hand panel. The perfection of the paradisal garden in the left-hand panel has become corrupted through lust and greed. The problem with this interpretation is that the central panel doesn't look like the consequences of the Fall. Everyone is naked, but no one is ashamed. No one is labouring through the sweat of their brows, and no woman is suffering the pain of childbirth (Genesis 3). In the late 1940s this panel was the centre of a new, libertarian interpretation of Bosch. Following the work of William Fraenger, a story was told of how the panel was commissioned by the grand master of the Adamites, a sect which believed that Eden was a paradise of free love, which could, and should, be practised by the initiated. Unhappily for those wistful for erotic precedents, there is not a shred of evidence for either the existence of the Adamites in the Brabant of Bosch's day or for his membership of such an organization. A more likely interpretation is that the sexual gambollers of the central panel are personifications of the principles of alchemy. Laurinda Dixon makes a convincing case for an alchemical reading by matching the strange structures of the panel with the instruments and vessels of the alchemist's laboratory. The couplings and cavortings are a painted metaphor for the processes of distillation and transmutation sought by the practical scientists of Bosch's day.

The right-hand panel is hell, its colour palette and its composition a world away from the pastoral beauty of Adam and Eve's marriage. Again, the alchemy motif is carried through: the curious monstrous man in the centre of the panel, sometimes referred to as the 'tree-man', was first identified by Jacques

Combe as being painted in the shape of an alchemist's egg retort: Combe named him the 'alchemical man'.

Just as the central panel is populated by finely detailed and convincingly realized characters, so too is hell populated. Here, though, the lusts and desires that controlled people while alive have been turned to the punishment of eternity: a woman guilty of vanity is forced to gaze upon the mirrored behind of one demon, while fondled by another. The glutton vomits, the avaricious man defecates gold coins, a musician has the demons' song tattooed to his backside.

We are fortunate that *The Garden of Earthly Delight* was not the subject of our journey. There is no painting in Renaissance art like it, and there is no painting like it for producing a multiplicity of interpretations, some more convincing than others. It is a painting that advocates sexual liberation, heretical teachings, astrological speculations, depicts Dutch proverbs or conveys coded messages from Cathars or to alchemists. Maybe so. Whatever the truth of its 'message', we cannot avoid the fact that it, above all his other paintings, characterizes Bosch's style for most people.

But we already have noticed that *Christ Mocked* is completely unlike, in conception and execution, the vision presented in *The Garden of Earthly Delight*. In *Christ Mocked* the focus of the artist, and the attention demanded of his viewer, is not on the spectacular, the pyrotechnic or the mysterious. Bosch achieves a much greater, and a much more important, thing: he makes us see, through the subtlety of his composition, the allusive nature of the objects and people depicted, the delicacy of his touch, that an event, historically completed once and for all in Palestine so long ago, is still being experienced and lived today. And this is the last circle in all our circles of thorns: a rippling circle on the surface of time, a circle from Christ's passion and redemption, whose meaning widens, and perhaps resonates, for ever.

Notes

1 This description of Bosch and his work is often ascribed to Carl Jung, although in the enormous collected works of the Swiss psychoanalyst there is no apparent reference to Bosch. Perhaps it is one of those things, like 'play it again, Sam', that *should have* been said. It is still a good summary of our painter.

2 Walter S. Gibson, *Hieronymus Bosch* (World of Art series; London: Thames & Hudson, 1973), p. 14.

3 See Bruno Blondé and Hans Vlieghe, 'The social status of Hieronymus Bosch', *The Burlington Magazine*, Vol. 131, No. 1039 (Oct., 1989), pp. 699–700.

4 Laurinda S. Dixon, *Bosch: Art & Ideas series* (London: Phaidon, 2003) p. 27.

5 Anthony Trollope, *The Warden* (1855). See especially Chapter 7, 'The Jupiter' (pp. 58–62 in the 1984 Penguin English Library edition).

6 Van Eyck, who was an early adopter, if not the inventor, of oil paints, used a recipe that mixed crushed glass and calcinated (baked) bones, boiled in linseed oil until thickened. It wasn't easy being a painter in those days!

7 Jeltje Dikstra, 'Technical Examination' in Bernhard Ridderbos, Anne van Buren and Henk van Veen, eds, *Early Netherlandish Paintings: Rediscovery, Reception and Research* (Los Angeles: The J. Paul Getty Museum, 2005), p. 304.

8 Van Mander, quoted in Dixon, *Bosch*, p. 35.

9 Erwin Panofsky, *Early Netherlandish Painting, its Origins and Character* (Cambridge MA: Harvard University Press, 1953), p. 151. Panofsky appropriated the term *ars nova* from another artistic medium, music, as he freely acknowledges. *Ars nova* was first coined in about 1320, by the composer Philippe de Vitry in a treatise of that name. In music *ars nova* was characterized by a suppler rhythmic sensibility compared with the triple metre, and complex and intricate notation of the preceding *ars antiqua*. De Vitry (1291–1361) and Guillaume de Machaut (c 1300–1377) are the most famous composers of the fourteenth-century *ars nova*. Panofsky claimed two Flemish composers of the next century as the pre-eminent exponents of musical *ars nova*: Guillaume Dufay (1400–74) and Gilles Binchois (c 1400–60).

10 Dixon, *Bosch*, p. 35.

Further Reading

It is one of the curiosities of our day and technology that it is perfectly possible to write about and hold strong opinions upon paintings that the writer has never seen in person, or even paintings that have not been together since leaving the artist's studio. The chief aid to this is, of course, the World Wide Web, and I must commend highly the 'Web Gallery of Art', a labour of love from a Hungarian physicist, Emil Krén. It is possible to view, at high resolutions, all of Bosch's paintings without the expense of travelling to Venice, Madrid, Lisbon et. al. I realize that nothing is an adequate substitute for viewing a painting in its real, physical presence: indeed, I hope that this whole book shows the worth that comes from a thoughtful, prayerful study of one particular painting! Even so, for the purposes of illustration then www.wga.hu/welcome.html can't be beaten.

The city of 's-Hertogenbosch prepared a website to accompany a major exhibition of Bosch's paintings held in Rotterdam in 2001. It has an excellent display of his life and work: www.boschuniverse. com. Unhappily it seems temperamental with any web browser other than Internet Explorer 6.

There are many books available on Bosch. Most seem to be swiftly produced reproductions of his more famous, fantastical works, with very little text. The best general introduction is by Laurinda S. Dixon, *Bosch*, in the Phaidon Art & Ideas series (London, 2003). It is generously illustrated, and contains a level-headed examination of some of the wilder recent ideas about Bosch and heresy. The latter strand is represented by Lynda Harris's *The Secret Heresy of Hieronymus Bosch* (Edinburgh: Floris Books, 1996), in which Bosch is portrayed as a Cathar, the one-size-fits-all heretics of *The Name of the Rose, Holy Blood and Holy Grail*, and, inevitably, *The*

DaVinci Code. Two, more sober, recent summaries of Bosch's life and works are found in *Hieronymus Bosch* (New York: Abbeville Press, 2006) by Larry Silver, a monumental and beautifully illustrated volume, and *Hieronymus Bosch: New insights into his life* (Rotterdam: Museum Boymans van Beuningen, 2001), edited by Bernard Vermet and Jos Koldeweij. This is the companion volume to the exhibition of Bosch's work shown at the Boijmans Van Beuningen Museum in Rotterdam in 2001. Its essays are illuminating; unfortunately all the illustrations are in muddy black and white: if you can't afford the Silver, you would need to buy the catalogue for the exhibition. A much older, but still valuable introduction to Bosch is in Walter S. Gibson's *Hieronymus Bosch* (London: Thames & Hudson, 1973) in the World of Art series.

Christ Mocked was shown at the National Gallery as part of the 'Seeing Salvation' exhibition in 2000. The exhibition catalogue, still available, gives a very good overview of the whole range of depictions of Jesus: Gabriele Finaldi, ed., *The Image of Christ* (London: National Gallery Publications, 2000). The only book I have discovered which looks in detail at *Christ Mocked* (books on Bosch's triptychs are almost ten a penny) is long out of print, which is a shame, because it is an excellent resource for learning how to read a number of paintings, and is the single most influential book on my reading of *Christ Mocked*: Richard Foster and Pamela Tudor-Craig, *The Secret Life of Paintings* (Woodbridge: Boydell Press, 1986). There are any number of articles in the art journals on Bosch, some of which I have referred to in the notes of each relevant chapter.

The definitive book of our generation on the history of religion in the lifetime of Hieronymus Bosch is Diarmaid MacCulloch's monumental, but very readable, *Reformation: Europe's House Divided, 1490–1700* (London: Allen Lane, 2003). For an even wider, general, history of Europe (getting away from the 'fog in Channel; continent cut off' attitude of old) look at Norman Davies's *Europe: A History* (Oxford: OUP, 1996). Davies is sometimes controversial in what he decides makes history, or finds interesting, but his ideas and interpretations are always stimulating.

The single best book on the cultural world of the late Middle Ages and Renaissance is C. S. Lewis's *The Discarded Image: An introduction to medieval and Renaissance literature* (Cambridge: CUP, 1964). Originally a lecture series given at Oxford University, in this book Lewis is able, in his characteristically lucid style, to tie together all the various strands of a world in which 'kyndely enclyning' was the dominant model of scientific thought. Lewis's contribution to the study of medieval thought is assessed in Norman F. Cantor's *Inventing the Middle Ages: The lives, works and ideas of the great medievalists of the twentieth century* (Cambridge: Lutterworth, 1992).

Rodney Stark writes very convincingly in favour of the social and scientific good of Christianity, and draws out the complexity of the political and religious forces at work in early modern Europe. His conclusions are unexpected (for example, witch burning was much more frequent and bloodier in parts of Europe where the power of the Church was weakened in the face of secular princes). The book to read is *For the Glory of God: How monotheism led to reformations, science, witch-hunts, and the end of slavery* (Princeton, NJ; Oxford: Princeton University Press, 2003).

A good introduction to the history of Christian mistreatment of Jews is found in Dan Cohn-Sherbok's *The Crucified Jew: Twenty centuries of Christian anti-semitism* (London: Fount Paperbacks, 1992).

The relationship between science and religion is best approached through the works of Alister McGrath and Keith Ward. The former's *Dawkins' God: Genes, memes and the meaning of life* (Oxford: Blackwell Publishing, 2005) is an excellent summary of Dawkins's scientific work, as even Dawkins himself says. It begins the work of refuting Dawkins's theological and metaphysical mistakes continued in *The Dawkins Delusion: Atheist fundamentalism and the denial of the divine* (London: SPCK, 2007), written by McGrath and his wife, Joanna Collicutt McGrath. If you own or read Richard Dawkins's *The God Delusion* (London: Bantam Press, 2006), do make sure you also read McGrath and McGrath. The most accessible book on the philosophical relationship between science and religion that Keith Ward has written recently is *Pascal's Fire: Scientific faith and religious understanding* (Oxford: OneWorld, 2006), although his *Is Religion Dangerous?* (Oxford: Lion Publishing, 2006) and the older *God, Chance and Necessity* (Oxford: OneWorld, 1996) are also worth reading. More technical books by the 'scientist-theologians' include Ian G. Barbour, *Religion and Science: Historical and contemporary issues* (London: SCM, 1998); John Polkinghorne *Belief in God in an Age of Science* (New Haven: Yale University Press, 1998), the same author's *Science and Christian Belief: Theological reflections of a bottom-up thinker* (London: SPCK, 1994); and Arthur Peacocke's *Paths from Science Towards God: The end of all our exploring* (Oxford: OneWorld, 2001).

Books on the New Monastic movement are still published relatively rarely in this country, although they are easily available through Amazon.com. A good place to start is Rutba House's *School(s) for Conversion: 12 Marks of a New Monasticism* (Eugene, OR: Cascade Books, 2005). They themselves remark on the strangeness of a book being edited by a house. They maintain a website, www.newmonastics.org, on which may be found a number of conference papers on the movement, and links to various newspaper and journal articles. Scott Bessenecker's *The New Friars: The emerging movement serving the world's poor*, is an inspiring account of Christian work and witness in 'the abandoned places of Empire' (Rutba House's phrase). *Making Room: Recovering hospitality as a Christian tradition* by Christine D. Pohl (Grand Rapids, MI: W.B. Eerdmans, 1999) explores the history and the present-day necessity of hospitality, as one of the signs of a Christian community. A surprising take on 'intentional communities' (as these communes are sometimes called) can be found in Tobias Jones's *Utopian Dreams* (London: Faber & Faber, 2007). It is surprising because it is a comparative work by a journalist, who found himself making value judgements about the communities he visited, and taking those values with him back into his life in the 'real world'. It is also elegantly written.

The standard book on the Brethren of the Common Life, by Hyma, is quite elderly now, and some of its assumptions about life and society in late medieval and early modern Europe have been superseded. The best way to understand the Brethren is to read their writings, and so I recommend John van Engen's edition of *Devotio Moderna: Basic writings* (Classics of Western Spirituality) (Mahwah, NJ: Paulist Press, 1988).

Etty Hillesum's writings are a revelation, for their vitality and wry humour, as well as the insight they provide into a shameful period of European history. There are two readily available editions of her diaries and letters. The more complete one is *Etty: The letters and diaries of Etty Hillesum, 1941–1943*, edited by Klaas Smelik, the son of the man to whom the diaries were originally entrusted (Grand Rapids: Eerdmans, 2002). A lightly condensed edition is the one I have quoted from, mainly because the production of the book, by Persephone Books, is so beautifully done. The girl who learnt to kneel deserves to have her words in a beautiful volume: *An Interrupted Life: The diaries and letters of Etty Hillesum, 1941–43*, translated by Arnold Pomerans (London: Persephone Books, 1999).

The best book on the Passion, the arrest, trial and execution of Jesus, is Raymond E. Brown's *The Death of the Messiah: From Gethsemane to the grave, a commentary on the Passion narratives in the four Gospels* (New York: Doubleday, 1994) in two massive volumes. If this is a little too detailed for you, then the same author's *A Crucified Christ in Holy Week* (Collegeville, MN: The Liturgical Press, 1986) is an excellent survey of the differences of fact and viewpoint in the four Gospel accounts. A more detailed look at the legal processes Jesus was subjected to can be found in Simon Légasse's *The Trial of Jesus* (London: SCM, 1997). The best book on the place of crucifixion in Roman, Greek and Jewish social history is Martin Hengel's *Crucifixion: In the ancient world and the folly of the message of the cross* (Philadelphia: Fortress Press, 1977).

Rowan Williams's *Tokens of Trust: An introduction to Christian belief* (Norwich: Canterbury Press, 2007) repays slow and meditative reading. I was present in Canterbury Cathedral for the original delivery of these talks, and they were a tour de force of concision and imagery.

Bill Viola's work is difficult to enjoy away from its original form. Video art doesn't make as good coffee table books as paintings do. Even so, the lavishly produced catalogue for the exhibition 'Going Forth by Day' is a good place to start: *Bill Viola: Going Forth by Day* (Berlin, New York: Guggenheim Museum Publications, 2002).

The music that emerged as a result of Eno's musing on muzak was originally released in 1978. It is now available on CD. Brian Eno, *Ambient 1: Music for Airports* (Virgin Records: ENOCD 6, 2004). Eno has produced four albums in the 'Ambient Series'. Additionally, and rather wonderfully, in 1983 he recorded a soundtrack album for a film that has never been released about the Apollo moon landing missions. There is a definite 'thickness/long now' feel to the music in *Apollo: Atmospheres and Soundtracks*, Brian Eno, Daniel Lanois and Roger Eno (Virgin Records, ENOCD 10, 2005).

Acknowledgements

It was Cyril Connolly who said that the enemy of any literary endeavour was the perambulator in the hall-way. If that is so (and I have an inkling he was right), then a greater enemy is depression. As I described in the Introduction, this book was the product of my recovery from a serious depression, both part of the therapy for my condition and a sign of its gradual amelioration. Something that helped, both depression and book, was the chance to escape the day-to-day responsibilities that confronted me in my own home. I found, through the kindness of friends and strangers, a number of bolt-holes as I recovered. The Sheldon Community in Devon took me in at the beginning of my illness and provided a loving silence around the noises of my emotions. Jeremy Davies and Simon McEnery gracefully gave me board, lodging, and broadband access, for a beautiful week in Salisbury Cathedral Close. The Dean and Chapter of Canterbury Cathedral, through the kindness and instigation of the former Archdeacon of Canterbury, Patrick Evans, provided me with rooms in the Cathedral International Study Centre, and access to the St Augustine's Library in the precincts, for two weeks over Passiontide, during which the bulk of the writing was accomplished. Other friends who allowed me rooms with a view (or without) were David and June-Mary Davies and Stephen Mason. To all of them, I am grateful.

The people of St Stephen's Church, Canterbury, allowed me as much space and time as I needed to recover my strength. In that period the churchwardens and the Ministry Leadership Team were marvels of discretion and loving inattention.

The burden of depression cannot be exaggerated, on the person experiencing it, but also, and possibly more acutely, on the family of the patient. My family, and especially my wife Siân, deserve public thanks and praise, for remaining, at the very least, my family and my wife during the weeks before the initial crisis of my illness and the long months of my recovery. Siân has, over almost 20 years of marriage, had to listen to many, many of my sermons, and has endured the frantic hours of sermon-deadlines. It is a pleasing thing to be able to offer this, in small recompense, something she hasn't heard before. And so, properly and lovingly, this work, of book and health, is dedicated to her.

Index

INDEX